The Quest For Equality

RT J. HARRIS

THE QUEST
FOR EQUALITY

The Constitution, Congress and
the Supreme Court

LOUISIANA STATE UNIVERSITY PRESS
BATON ROUGE

83893

For two hardy octogenarians,

my mother, Lucy Talley Harris,

and

my mentor, Edward S. Corwin.

Preface

SOME MONTHS BEFORE THE DECISION
of the Supreme Court in the Public School Segregations Cases
I began sporadic investigations of the judicial interpretation
of the "equal protection" clause of the federal Constitution
and a year after the decision resumed these studies with a
view to writing a history of the theoretical and constitutional
origins, congressional background, and judicial application
of the constitutional prohibition that no state "shall deny to
any person within its jurisdiction the equal protection of the
laws." In April, 1959, results of these investigations were
used in the Edward Douglass White Lectures at Louisiana
State University. With some modifications the present volume
is an outgrowth of those lectures within the context in which
they were actually delivered. Accordingly, the study is not a
complete history of the equal protection clause as originally
contemplated, but an attempt to relate the origins of "the
equal protection of the laws" in political theory and the landmarks of Anglo-American constitutionalism to its legislative
history in the 39th Congress which proposed the amendment
and in succeeding sessions of Congress through 1875 when the
last federal statute to implement the clause was enacted, and

upon these foundations to lay the judicial interpretation of equal protection.

For so little a volume great and numerous obligations have been incurred. It is a pleasure to express gratitude to the Institute of Research in the Social Sciences of Vanderbilt University for generous summer grants for conducting the initial studies and to my friends and colleagues of the Department of Government and the Law School of Louisiana State University for the invitation to give the White Lectures and for the pleasant treatment accorded to me while I was in their benign and gentle custody for almost a week. I am heavily indebted to Professors Alpheus T. Mason, Carl B. Swisher, René deVisme Williamson, and William C. Havard, Jr., for reading the manuscript and offering many useful suggestions.

Expressions of appreciation are due to my wife, Dashiel B. Harris, for her correction of manuscript and proof; Mrs. Cleo Wescoat Sandlin for typing the draft used for the lectures; Mrs. Anna B. Luton for typing the final manuscript; and Mrs. Audrey Riven Adler for research assistance and checking of sources. The responsibility for contents and conclusions and any errors therein are exclusively mine. Finally, I wish to express appreciation to the *Temple Law Quarterly* for permission to reproduce with a few changes in Chapters IV and VI most of my article, "The Constitution, Education, and Segregation," 29 *Temple Law Quarterly,* 409 (1956), to Harcourt, Brace and Company for permission to quote a passage from Clinton Rossiter's *Seedtime of the Republic,* and to Alfred A. Knopf, Inc., for permission to quote some sentences from Professor Phillips Bradley's edition of Alexis de Tocqueville's *Democracy in America.*

Robert J. Harris

Nashville, Tennessee
April, 1960

Table of Contents

Introduction

IN A NUMBER OF WAYS THE FOUR-
teenth Amendment to the American Constitution has persistently been one of the most controversial articles, not only
among legislators, executives, and judges, but also among
scholars in constitutional law and history. The circumstances
of its proposal by Congress and its ratification by the states
provoked bitter disputes, and arguments were seriously made
that the amendment was neither validly proposed nor
adopted. When the controversy over submission and ratification subsided, equally serious disputes arose with respect to
the meaning of its various provisions. Although controversial
at their inception the meaning of the second, third, and
fourth sections has hardly been a matter for dispute, nor
have these sections been of enduring importance.

The second section provides for the proportional reduction
of the representation in Congress of those states which abridge
the suffrage of adult male citizens except for participation in
rebellion or other crime, and it was obviously intended as an
indirect device to enfranchise Negroes and as a direct means
of preventing the states of the former Confederacy from gain-
ing representation under the section's repeal of the provision
counting three-fifths of the slaves for purposes of representa-

tion. Moreover, this section has never been implemented despite systematic exclusion by state laws of adult male citizens from the suffrage, either because Congress has lacked the will to enforce it, or because the committee system in both houses or the rules of procedure in the Senate render effective enforcement legislation impossible or politically unfeasible.

The third section disqualified for all public offices and disfranchised all former confederates who had served in any civil or military office in a state or the United States prior to the Civil War, subject to the power of Congress to remove such disabilities by a two-thirds vote of each house. The meaning and purpose of this section are also clear. However, this section lost its significance as Congress progressively removed the disabilities of all former Rebels except a few of the outstanding leaders who remained mute political symbols of the idea that an unsuccessful attempt to overthrow the government of the United States by force, violence, and other illegal means is not politically profitable. The fourth section unnecessarily validated the public debt of the United States incurred in prosecuting the Civil War and also prohibited the United States or any state from paying any portion of the Confederate debt or from giving compensation for the emancipation of slaves. Like the immediately preceding section, this section is obsolete.

Though not obsolete, the fifth section, which empowers Congress "to enforce, by appropriate legislation the provisions of this article," has fallen into desuetude, because no legislation has been enacted in pursuance of the power conferred since the Civil Rights Act of 1875. However, proposed legislation in the form of antilynching bills, laws to enforce court orders in public school segregation cases, and the like provide ample reminders of the existence of the fifth section and give to it enough vitality to arouse the fears and anger of white supremacists and extreme advocates of states' rights in all matters where individual rights are concerned.

During the first ninety-one years of the existence of the Fourteenth Amendment the only provisions of great practical importance were contained in the first section, which defines citizenship in the United States and provides that "no state shall make or enforce any law which shall abridge the privileges or immunities of citizens of the United States; nor shall any state deprive any person of life, liberty or property without due process of law; nor deny to any person within its jurisdiction the equal protection of the laws." All of these prohibitions, and especially that of the equal protection clause, have a long background in the principles of the law of citizenship or nationality, Magna Carta, and the law of nature as conceived by the Stoics in Greece and Rome and as transmitted by the Christian Fathers, the democratic philosophers of the seventeenth and eighteenth centuries, and American state constitutions until the Abolitionists and Radical Republicans endeavored to apply them to former slaves in the nineteenth century.

Scholarly and juridical controversies have long raged over the meaning of the first section of the Amendment, either standing alone or read in conjunction with the fifth section. For the most part these disputes revolved about the due process clause because of the unwarranted judicial primacy accorded to it by the Supreme Court between 1887 and 1937 in matters affecting property and between 1925 and 1960 in matters affecting the guarantees of the Bill of Rights as limits on state action. Accordingly, the equal protection clause has been of secondary importance at least until 1954, as contrasted with the judicial distention of due process of law and the judicial emaciation of the privileges and immunities clause. Even so, equal protection has been an important constitutional concept in varying degrees since the ratification of the Fourteenth Amendment in 1868.

In its interpretation of the equal protection clause the Supreme Court has given almost no attention to the theoretical and legal origins of the dual concept of equality and protection, to the debates in the 39th Congress over the proposal of the Fourteenth Amendment, or the conditions which the framers of the Amendment sought to change or rectify. Indeed, it has almost read the word "protection" out of the clause so as to confine its meaning to equality before the law, narrowly interpreted to mean state or official action in the making and administering of laws. Simultaneously it has assumed for itself the power originally vested in Congress to enforce the Amendment. For these reasons a cursory examination of the historical development of the ideas of equality and protection, the legislative history of the equal protection clause, and judicial interpretation of it provide an interesting contrast between dream and fulfilment, ideal and reality, and legislative intent and judicial construction.

The Quest For Equality

CHAPTER ONE

The American Tradition
of Equality

IMPLICIT AND EXPLICIT IN THE PRO-
hibition of the Fourteenth Amendment that no state "shall
deny to any person within its jurisdiction the equal protection of the laws" are two ideas: (1) the duty of government to
protect all persons in their civil rights and (2) the equality
of all persons before the law.

The idea of protection has a long background in the ancient
principle of the feudal law and the later law of citizenship
that in return for allegiance the lord or government respectively owes protection to the vassal, subject, or citizen.
The idea is also grounded in the philosophy of John Locke
and other theorists of the social compact who asserted that by
the social compact men did not surrender all of their rights
to government, but only some of them in order better to
protect the unalienable rights of person and property which
they retained. The Lockean conception of government as a
device for the protection of unalienable rights was a cardinal
doctrine of American Revolutionary political theory which
culminated in the Declaration of Independence. In one suc-
cinct passage Jefferson distilled volumes of political theory,

some of which had its origins in Grecian Stoic philosophy, was advanced and preserved by Roman jurists and publicists and the Christian Fathers, and transmitted to Anglo-American jurisprudence by Richard Hooker, Locke, and others. The passage runs: "We hold these truths to be self-evident, That all men are created equal, that they are endowed by their creator with certain unalienable rights; that among these are life, liberty, & the pursuit of happiness; that to secure these rights governments are instituted among men, deriving their just powers from the consent of the governed."

Here and in the succeeding sentiments are most of the elements of Western democratic theory: (1) equality, (2) unalienable rights, (3) the institution of government to protect these rights, (4) government by the consent of the governed, and (5) the right of the people to change government either by peaceable means or by revolution.

The equal protection clause involves only two of these elements: (1) the duty of government to protect the rights of life, liberty, and personal security generally, and (2) the equality of all persons before the law. Important as it is in Western political and legal thought, the concept of protection is much less difficult than that of equality and has been far less subject to change in its content. Feudal law recognized a series of mutual rights and obligations of a contractual nature between lord and vassal, rights and obligations which were enforceable in the feudal courts. Among other obligations, lord and vassal reciprocally owed each other protection of body and possessions. The vassal owed loyalty and obedience to his lord, the lord owed justice to the vassal. Thus, according to the Assizes of the Court of Burgesses of Jerusalem, the king took an oath to protect both the poor and the rich in the exercise of their rights, just as United States Supreme Court justices later took an oath to "do equal justice to the poor and to the rich." Similar thoughts are found in the writings of Henry of Bracton and Ranulf de Glanville.

The right of the vassal or subject to protection from the king was elevated to the dignity of a constitutional principle by Magna Carta. In the fortieth clause King John promised: "To no one will we sell, to no one will we deny right or justice." The expression is negative, but the meaning is affirmative. In the evolution of Magna Carta all became entitled to right and justice without delay or purchase. Because of the contractual nature of feudal rights and obligations, a violation of rights by lord or vassal absolved the other of his obligations. If the lord withheld protection, he forfeited allegiance; if the vassal failed in obedience, he forfeited his fief and became an outlaw.[1] Protection and security against violence and other wrongs as prime objectives of government were equally the theme of Thomas Hobbes and John Locke in their disparate ways, and the parallel between the principles of feudal law and Locke's conceptions of the reciprocal nature of protection and allegiance is obvious. Locke made the chief end of the social compact the preservation of property, broadly construed to include rights of personal liberty. Hence when man entered into a social compact he was to enjoy many conveniences, including protection "of himself, his liberty, and property," by the whole strength of civil society.[2]

Thus from a blending of feudal law and the principles of the social compact there emerged the principle of Western constitutionalism which asserts that it is the duty of government to protect all persons under standing and general laws

[1] On this subject see A. J. Carlyle, *A History of Mediaeval Political Theory in the West* (6 vols., London, 1928–1936), III, 27, 33–35, 53, 64–65, 79, 164, 167, 185; Bracton (Henry of Bratton), *De Legibus et Consuetudinibus Angliae*, ed. George E. Woodbine (4 vols., New Haven, 1942), ii, 35.2 (fol. 78), iii, 7.1 (fol. 5); Glanville (Ranulf de), *Tractatus de Legibus Consuetudinibus Regni Angliae*, ed. John Rayner (London, 1780).

[2] John Locke, *The Second Treatise on Civil Government* ("Blackwell's Political Texts" [Oxford, 1948]), 62, 64. Despite his elimination of a contractual relationship between sovereign and subject, Hobbes is as emphatic as any writer in designating protection and security of person as a primary end of government. See *Leviathan* ("Blackwell's Political Texts" [Oxford, 1946]), 109.

impartially administered by upright judges. The right to
protection is not confined to citizens. Locke clearly recognized the right of aliens or persons not within the social compact to protection, and both municipal law and international
law have long recognized the rights of aliens to be protected
and treated according to minimum standards of civilized
justice.

The idea of equality is more difficult and has a longer
history. Equality is at least coeval with if not prior to liberty
in the history of Western political thought, and among the
Greek and Roman Stoics and the Christian Fathers it was a
far more important concept. Like liberty, equality has its
history and its varying connotations. To the Stoics it meant
the equality of all men by nature as distinguished from convention. To the Christian Fathers it connoted the spiritual
equality of all persons in Jesus Christ despite temporal inequalities. To subsequent democratic theorists it meant the
political and legal equality of all men, as distinguished from
physical qualities, material wealth, and social position. To
the Jacksonian Democracy it meant the abolition of special
privileges, the elimination of monopolies, equality of economic opportunity, universal manhood suffrage, and the
right of citizens to share equally in office. To none of its
proponents has equality connoted identity. On the contrary,
the basic assumption of all equalitarians is the uniqueness and
essential worth and dignity of all human beings as individual
persons. Regardless of such differences, however, all men are
endowed with reason, capable of attaining virtue, and equally
entitled as members of the human race, to recognition of certain rights.

Between 301 B.C., when "that gaunt, tall and swarthy
figure" known as Zeno the Stoic [3] broke with the Aristotelian
view of the natural inequality of men to proclaim the equality of all men under an all pervasive law of nature, and the

[3] Sir Ernest Barker, *Alexander to Constantine* (Oxford, 1956), 21.

decision of the Supreme Court of the United States in the Public School Segregation Cases is a vast gulf in time and distance. However, these remote and disparate events proceed from the common theme of the equality of all men, the brotherhood of man, and the essential unity of the human race, although for different reasons. The Stoics' rejection of the city-state for cosmopolitanism and inequality for equality under universal law represents one of the great landmarks in Western political theory which was to influence the laws and institutions of Rome and its successors.[4]

In Rome, where Stoic principles found a congenial home, Cicero was one of the more articulate exponents of the natural equality of all men under an immutable and universal law of nature. His lack of originality even enhances the importance of his doctrines as the commonplace sentiments of the Rome of his period. Cicero began his discussion of liberty by proclaiming that liberty can abide only in those states in which the people have supreme power and in which liberty is equally enjoyed by all citizens. Liberty and equality were thus made indispensable complements to each other instead of possible opposites, which has been the fashion of some later writers. Cicero also emphasized that voting alone is not enough to make a government a commonwealth or, as we would say, a democracy, unless men are actually free and equal, and therefore eligible to all the offices of government. Moreover, since equality of rights is a part of the law that holds political society together, all citizens "of the same commonwealth ought to enjoy equal rights in their mutual relations." [5]

In the *De Legibus* Cicero grounds the equality of men upon reason implanted in man by God. Because all men possess reason and are capable of attaining wisdom and virtue

[4] See Carlyle, *A History of Mediaeval Political Theory in the West*, I, 7–8.
[5] Marcus Tullius Cicero, "On the Commonwealth," *De Re Publica*, trans. George H. Sabine and Stanley B. Smith (Columbus, Ohio, 1929), Book I, Parts XXXI–XXXII.

"there is no difference in kind between man and man," and one definition of man is applicable to all men. Not only is reason common to all men, but "the same things are invariably perceived by the senses," and speech, though it may differ in the choice of words, speaks the same language. The similarity of the human race is also clearly visible in its evil as in its good tendencies. Pleasure attracts and pain repels all men. We shun death and cling to life. "Troubles, joys, desires, and fears harried the minds of all men without distinction, and even if different men have different beliefs, that does not prove for example that it is not the same quality of superstition that besets some races which worship cats as gods, as that which torments other races." Inasmuch, therefore, as "the human race is bound together in unity, it follows, finally, that knowledge of the principles of right living is what makes men better." [6]

Although Cicero stated his theories of natural law and equality clearly, he was concerned neither with the inconsistency of his views with the brutal facts of objective reality, such as slavery, nor with the consequences of his doctrines. Indeed, Cicero was hardly an equalitarian in the modern sense because the general emphasis of his writings is upon an aristocracy of the wise and the virtuous. However, in regarding all men as endowed with reason and as capable of attaining virtue, Cicero made a major contribution to the development of equality as a political, legal, and ethical principle. This lack of an analysis of theory as related to practice was supplied by Seneca, who repeated at length and in greater detail the traditional views of the Stoics on equality and then went on to analyze slavery. Virtue, to him, is attainable by all, the free and the slave, the king and the exile. A slave can be as virtuous and as noble as his master because it is fortune that makes man a slave. Slavery is odious to all

[6] *On the Laws in "De Re Publica" and "De Legibus,"* trans. Clinton W. Keyes ("Loeb Classical Library" [Cambridge, Mass., 1928]), Book I, Parts X, XI.

men and is external only, in that it applies only to the body, never to the mind. Slavery, therefore, exists by convention and not by nature. Seneca resolved the conflict between convention and nature by postulating a golden age or primitive state in which all men were innocent, though ignorant, and lived happily in peace and shared all things in common. However, in the course of time this primitive innocence disappeared with the advent of avarice, so that conventional social and political institutions emerged as the result of vice and the corruption of human nature. Slavery and other kinds of inequality were the results of defects in human nature or, in Thomas Paine's phrase, "the badge of lost innocence." [7]

If political philosophy be a process of continuous development, as the Carlyles and Charles H. McIlwain have persuasively demonstrated that it is, it is difficult to overestimate the contributions of the Stoics, which reached their culmination in the writings of Cicero and Seneca. In their teachings are to be found most of the elements of modern democratic philosophy—the essential worth and dignity of the individual person, the rationality of man, the equality of all men, natural liberty, and the consent of the governed. In this sense, therefore, the Stoics broke away from antiquity and initiated the Western political tradition as subsequently extolled by Locke and the American Revolutionary Fathers. All that was needed was a vehicle for bearing these traditions until they should be translated into political reality.

As it happened, two vehicles appeared. The first was the Roman law as reflected by the writings of great jurisconsults like Ulpian, Papinian, and Modestinus, among others, who infused Stoic principles into Roman jurisprudence. Thus Ulpian, while recognizing slavery as sanctioned by the *jus gentium,* asserted that by the law of nature all men are born free and equal, and applied this concept to slavery, marriage, property, and other legal institutions to mitigate the sub-

[7] See Carlyle, *A History of Mediaeval Political Theory in the West,* I, 20–24, 27.

8   THE QUEST FOR EQUALITY

merged status of slaves and married women before the law.[8]
The second vehicle was the early and mediaeval Christian
Church, which not only kept these traditions alive but gave
to them some new applications. For obvious reasons such
Stoic conceptions as an original golden age or paradise, the
equality of all men, the unity of mankind, and the subsequent
corruption of human nature were congenial to the Christian
Fathers. The paradise in Eden, the primitive innocence of
Adam and Eve, the uninvited but apparently welcome intru-
sion of the serpent, the fall of man, and the advent of sin
which made civil institutions necessary to curb the evil in
all men are close parallels to Stoic philosophy, and in particular to that of Seneca. More important is the conception
of the equality of all men as descended from common
ancestors and the fatherhood of God as the maker of heaven
and earth and all things visible and invisible.

It is no wonder therefore that St. Paul should proclaim the
equality of all men in the communion of the universal
Church, so that "there is neither Jew nor Greek, there is
neither bond nor free, there is neither male nor female: for
ye are all one in Christ Jesus." [9] Similarly, in Colossians
"there is neither Greek nor Jew . . . barbarian, Scythian,
bond nor free: but Christ is all, and in all." [10] As Sir Ernest
Barker says, any Stoic could have made these statements, but
no Stoic, he continues, could have said what St. Paul wrote
in the first Epistle to the Corinthians, when he virtually
abolished the distinction between the wise and the foolish
of this world to conclude "that not many wise men after the
flesh, not many mighty, not many noble, are called; but God
chose the foolish things of the world, that he might put to
shame them that are wise," and chose the weak to confound
the mighty.[11]

[8] *Ibid.*, 39, 47; *Corpus Juris, Civilis, Digesta*, ed. Theodor Mommsen (Berlin,
  1868–1870), i 1.4, 1.17, 32.
[9] Gal. 3:28.   [10] Col. 3:11.
[11] I Cor. 1:26–28; Barker, *Alexander to Constantine*, 401.

To be sure, the teachings of St. Paul and the Christian Fathers bearing upon the equality of all men in Christ or in the sight of God as creatures made in his image involve a dualism between the city of God and the city of man as exemplified later by St. Augustine, and were not applicable to a world corrupted by sin which made civil institutions necessary. The church Fathers unanimously expounded the doctrine that all men are by nature free and equal, while condoning slavery and other distinctions as conventions made necessary by the advent of sin. All men are the children of God, endowed with reason and capable of virtue. Equality is a spiritual, not a secular or temporal matter, and therefore is not of this world.[12] Nevertheless, their ideas of equality could easily be translated into secular and temporal affairs. If men were equal in God's sight, why, after all, should there be distinctions among human beings in this world?

From the Stoics to the Christian Fathers and thence to Locke, who is at least the godfather of American democratic thought, runs a continuous thread of political philosophy which, though it may vary in detail with respect to human nature, emphatically asserts the unity of mankind and the equality of all men. Because of Locke's influence on American political ideas from the Declaration of Independence to the present, independently of his theories of majority rule, legislative supremacy, and materialistic psychology, his conception of equality is of the utmost significance.

In describing his postulated state of nature, Locke stressed the perfect equality and perfect freedom of all men under the laws of nature as self-evident, and beyond question all men are creatures "of the same species and rank, promiscuously born to all the same advantages of nature, and the use of the same faculties."[13] Though all men are by nature equal,

[12] Carlyle, *A History of Mediaeval Political Theory in the West*, I, 113–20, 127, 131. Among the more important figures cited and quoted by Carlyle are Lactantius, St. Gregory the Great, St. Augustine, and St. Isidore of Seville.
[13] Locke, *The Second Treatise on Civil Government*, 4.

Locke made it clear that he did not mean identity or all kinds of equality and that God might set some men above others. Age, virtue, merit, and birth may set some apart from others, but all this, he asserted, is not inconsistent with the equality of all men with respect to jurisdiction or dominion of one over another, because every man has an equal right to his natural freedom.[14] Children are not born in a full state of equality; rather they are born to it and attain it upon maturity. Similarly, idiots, lunatics, and others who lack reason because of defects of nature occupy a special status. Slavery, however, is a species of war against nature, because man who was born perfectly free and equal cannot be put under the dominion of another save by his own consent. Even then he cannot subject himself to the arbitrary power of another. There are limits, therefore, to legislative and governmental power, so that with respect to equality rulers "are to govern by promulgated established laws, not to be varied in particular cases, but to have one rule for rich and poor, for the favorite at court and the countryman at plough." [15] Finally, Locke stressed fair and equal representation on the basis of population as distinguished from geographical units.

Although we do not usually associate Hobbes and the orthodox Puritans either with each other or with champions of democratic thought, both in their own ways, which are somewhat parallel, contributed significantly to the theory of equality without always advocating it socially or politically. Whereas the political theory of the Stoics, the early Christians, and Locke was optimistic concerning human nature, Hobbes and the Puritans were pessimistic. "Nature," says Hobbes, "hath made men so equal, in the faculties of the body, and mind; as that though there be found one man sometimes manifestly stronger of body, or of quicker mind than another; yet when all is reckoned together, the difference between man, and man, is not so considerable, as that one man can there-

[14] *Ibid.,* 28.   [15] *Ibid.,* 71.

upon claim to himself any benefit, to which another may not pretend, as well as he." With respect to physical strength the weakest can kill the strongest either by stealth or with the aid of others. Regarding the faculties of the mind there is an even greater equality among men, "for prudence, is but experience, which equal time equally bestows on all men, in those things they equally apply themselves unto." [16]

Without a conscious design the Puritans of England and colonial New England contributed to the diffusion of equalitarian sentiments. First, under the dogma of the total depravity of man the Calvinistic Puritans enunciated the idea that all men are equal in sin and equally unworthy of God's love. Second, under the dogma of predestination they advanced the doctrine of the elect few who would be chosen by God's grace for salvation. Although this dogma made for a rigorous distinction between the elect and the damned, saints and sinners, it simultaneously held that no man can save himself and that one man's chance for salvation is as good as another's. If all men are equal in sin, or in the aristocracy of Christian grace, it is no great inference to say that they are also equal in other respects. Moreover, if everyone's chances are equal in what could uncritically be called a rigged lottery for salvation, then it is easy to infer that men are equal in other ways as well.[17]

Even so, Puritan conceptions of equality were theological and were independent of rank and wealth in this world. Consequently the idea of the equality or the priesthood of all believers affirms the inferiority of all others. However, as Professor Woodhouse has indicated, the Puritans had to accept a degree of practical equality in their struggle for their own religious liberty. The Puritans of the Left soon discovered that guarantees of the liberty of the saint are in-

[16] Hobbes, Leviathan, 80.
[17] For an excellent account of the contribution of Puritanism to equality, see William Haller, The Rise of Puritanism ("Torchbooks" series [New York, 1957]), 12, 86, 153, 169, 178, 203, 205, 268.

effective unless the liberty of the sinner is equally guaranteed.[18] In another respect Puritanism, which was not a monolithic theology or movement, contributed to the philosophy of equality. Among the Separatists and Independents there were levelling and radical elements both in Cromwell's army and in New England. Colonel Thomas Rainborough and his fellow Levellers made the most emphatic demands for political equality and universal male suffrage on the basis of natural rights and natural law. To Rainborough the poorest in England has a life to live, as does the richest, and if a man is to live under a government he must by his own consent put himself under that government.[19] Moreover, there was a tendency among the Levellers to equate political liberty and political equality as indispensable complements to each other, just as the Roman Stoics and Christian Fathers tended to equate liberty and equality.

Despite the existence of teachings and practices of inequality in colonial America, doctrines of equality flourished there. In Rhode Island Roger Williams both preached and practiced equality of religions, cultures, and nationalities with respect to Indians, Jews, Papists, pagans, and indeed all except the nudist Quakers, whose conduct, as distinguished from their beliefs, had to be suppressed. Just as important, he advanced the idea of equality of the right to own land, which at that time meant equality of economic opportunity, equality in law and in government. Williams' theories of equality were grounded both in Puritan theology and in the difficult conditions which confronted him at the time of his banishment from Massachusetts and his subsequent efforts to construct a Christian commonwealth in Rhode Island.[20]

[18] A. S. P. Woodhouse (ed.), *Puritanism and Liberty, Being the Army Debates (1647–9) from the Clarke Manuscripts with Supplementary Documents* (London, 1950), [13, 53, 81].
[19] *Ibid.*, 53. See also in the same volume the second "Agreement of the People" of 1648, for an emphasis on the application of the law to all persons without favor or exemption (pp. 362–63).
[20] Perry Miller, *Roger Williams* (Indianapolis and New York, 1953), 51, 54, 139,

Although they are more spontaneous, his writings lack the studious background characteristic of John Wise's *Vindication of the Government of the New England Churches,* which appeared in 1717. Quoting almost verbatim from Baron Samuel Pufendorf, Wise enumerated three capital immunities in man's nature: (1) that "he is most properly the subject of the law of nature" as the "favorite of God's creatures"; (2) that man has "an original liberty stamped upon his rational nature"; (3) that there is "an equality among men which is not to be denied by the law of nature till man has resigned himself with all his rights for the sake of a civil state." Even then, his personal liberty and equality are "to be cherished, and preserved to the highest degree" consistent with just distinctions among men of honor and the public good.[21] Man has an individual worth and dignity, and it is a command of the law of nature "that every man esteem another as one who is naturally his equal, or who is a man as well as he." All men are descended from a common father, their bodies are composed of the same matter, all owe their existence to the same method of propagation. "The noblest mortal, in his entrance onto the stage of life, is not distinguished by any pomp or of passage from the lowest of mankind; and our life hastens to the same general mark: death observes no ceremony, but knocks as loud at the barriers of the court as at the door of the cottage." [22]

As a skeptic and a practical man of many affairs, Benjamin Franklin had little time for the abstractions which Wise borrowed from Pufendorf and he had little interest in natural law as "a brooding omnipresence in the sky." On

---

159, 173, 222; Clinton Rossiter, *Seedtime of the Republic* (New York, 1953), 202.

[21] *A Vindication of the Government of the New England Churches* (Gainesville, Fla., 1950), 34, 37, 39.

[22] *Ibid.,* 40–41. For Wise's quotation from Pufendorf in these passages, with or without any indication of it, see Charles A. Cook, *John Wise, Early American Democrat* (New York, 1952), 135–39. See also Baron Samuel Pufendorf, *De Jure Naturae et Gentium* (1672; English translation, London, 1703).

purely practical grounds, therefore, he emphasized the personal securities of life and liberty and the equal claim to them of the poorest "whatever Difference Time, Chance, or Industry may occasion in their Circumstances." [23] Accordingly, he opposed such devices of political inequality as property qualifications for voting and a second legislative chamber to check the actions of a popular representative assembly. Because "the *all* of one man is as dear to him as the *all* of another . . . the poor man has an *equal* right but *more* need to have representatives in the legislature than the rich one." [24]

Liberty and equality were the twin themes of the American Revolution. According to James Wilson all men "are, by nature, equal and free," and "no one has a right to authority over another without his consent." As Professor Rossiter says: "Revolutionary thinkers were in virtually unanimous accord on this point. Men might be grossly unequal in appearance, talents, intelligence, virtue, and fortune, but to this extent at least they were absolutely equal: No man had any natural right of dominion over any other; every man was free in the sight of God and plan of nature. The ranks and privileges of organized society were the result of unnatural usurpation, faulty institutions, the dead hand of the ignorant past, or the inevitable division of men into rulers and ruled." [25] In this sense equality was not absolute and did not imply identity. All men were equally free, equality and liberty were inseparable, and it was the task of government to reduce artificial inequalities to a minimum. To Samuel Adams, that prince of revolutionaries, but no leveller, equality in liberty was both more attainable and more necessary than equality in property, in the sense that liberty cannot be preserved unless all people possess it equally.

[23] Rossiter, *Seedtime of the Republic,* 292.
[24] *Ibid.,* 293. See A. H. Smyth (ed.), *The Writings of Benjamin Franklin* (10 vols., New York, 1905–1907), X, 59–60, 130–31.
[25] Rossiter, *Seedtime of the Republic,* 374.

Revolutionary ideas of equality culminated in the Virginia Declaration of Rights and the Declaration of Independence. In the former it is asserted that "all men are by nature equally free and independent, and have certain inherent rights, of which, when they enter into a state of society, they cannot by any compact deprive or divest their posterity." Similarly, because religion can only be directed by reason and conviction, "all men are equally entitled to the free exercise" of it. The Declaration of Independence is more sweeping. "All men are created equal." Jefferson states no qualifications and makes no exceptions. All are in turn endowed with certain unalienable rights by the law of nature and nature's God. Government is formed by the consent of the governed to protect these rights, and when it becomes subversive of them, it is the right of the people to alter or abolish it. The Declaration is simultaneously a summary of the Western democratic tradition and a ringing proclamation of the American political and secular faith.

To be sure, Jefferson, like the faithful of all ages, had doubts which troubled him. His emphasis upon the physical and other differences between Negroes and Caucasians in the *Notes on Virginia* [26] makes clear that he believed the Negro to be inferior to the white and the Indian not only in reason and imagination but in other qualities as well. However, he desired to believe in Negro equality and was jubilant when his correspondents sent him evidence of it.[27] His doubts of Negro equality, according to his own explanation or apology, were "the result of personal observation on the limited sphere of my own State, where the opportunities for the development of their genius were not favorable, and those exercising it still less so." [28] Moreover, because Sir Isaac New-

[26] Reprinted in Adrienne Koch and William Peden, *The Life and Selected Writings of Thomas Jefferson* (New York, 1944), 256–62.
[27] Letter to Benjamin Banneker, August 30, 1791, *ibid.*, 508–509; and to M. Henri Gregoire, February 25, 1809, *ibid.*, 594–95.
[28] Letter to Gregoire, *ibid.*

ton was superior to other men in understanding "he was not therefore lord of the person or property of others." Regardless of all doubts concerning intrinsic equality, Jefferson never wavered in his abhorrence of slavery and his belief in the equal right of all men to freedom under law.

Despite any qualifications concerning intrinsic equality, his repeated emphasis upon a natural aristocracy of talent and virtue, and other qualifications that could be noted, Jefferson belongs in the front ranks of those who have contributed to the American tradition of equality. His hatred for slavery and all artificial privileges and distinctions, his program of land for the landless and free education for the poor, his belief in the educability and improvement of all men, and his conception of equality in political representation and a qualified extension of the suffrage represent in their respective ways a kind of equality before the law, equality of opportunity, and equality in government. He thereby laid the foundations upon which the Jacksonian Democracy and subsequent successors were to build.[29]

Although the Jacksonian Democracy lacked a central spokesman and Andrew Jackson was largely immune to the political speculation so characteristic of Jefferson, it, nevertheless, made substantial contributions to the theory and practice of equality. In state legislation designed to protect labor, in judicial decisions and statutes curbing corporations, monopolies, and special privilege, and in their emphasis upon the equal rights of men to vote and hold office the Jacksonians translated theory into material accomplishment. Moreover, when occasion demanded it Jackson and his followers could eloquently articulate the premises of equality, its scope, and its limitations. Thus in his celebrated veto of the bank bill Jackson declaimed that "the rich and powerful too often bend

[29] On these subjects see Charles M. Wiltse, *The Jeffersonian Tradition in American Democracy* (Chapel Hill, 1935), 82–83, 101, 104, 136–44, 212; Dumas Malone, *Jefferson and His Time* (2 vols., Boston, 1948, 1951), I, 177, 239, 253, 257, 283, 379, 381, 415; II, 129, 157.

the acts of government to their selfish purposes." Then he continued: "Distinctions in society will always exist under every just government. Equality of talents, of education, or of wealth can not be produced by human institutions. In the full enjoyment of the gifts of Heaven and the fruits of superior industry, economy, and virtue, every man is equally entitled to protection by law; but when the laws undertake to add to these natural and just advantages artificial distinctions, to grant titles, gratuities, and exclusive privileges, to make the rich richer, and the potent more powerful, the humble members of society—the farmers, mechanics, and laborers—who have neither the time nor the means of securing like favors to themselves, have a right to complain of the injustice of their Government. There are no necessary evils in government. Its evils exist only in its abuses. If it would confine itself to equal protection, and, as Heaven does its rains, shower its favors alike on the high and the low, the rich and the poor, it would be an unqualified blessing." [30] Here, in positive terms, is a complete formulation of the equal right of all persons to the equal protection of equal laws in phrases that are almost identical to the negative version in the Fourteenth Amendment which was proposed thirty-four years later.

Aside from exceptions like the Locofocos, Jacksonian Democrats did not include the Negro in their equalitarian schemes. Indeed, some of them like Jackson himself were slave owners, and others had no objection to slavery. Until the rise of the Abolitionists the omission of the Negro from theories of equality in American thought was commonplace, based on the assumption either that the Negro was not a full man or that equality was a canon of perfection not attainable in objective reality. It was the Abolitionists, therefore, who revitalized doctrines of equality and natural rights under a

[30] James D. Richardson, *Messages and Papers of the Presidents* (10 vols., New York, 1904), II, 590.

literal interpretation of the Declaration of Independence
which applied to all men, black or white, and made slavery
a nullity as a violation of the laws of nature. Otherwise the
Abolitionists said little of equality that had not been said
before. Even so, their influence is of the utmost importance
because from their theories of racial equality, liberty, and
natural rights emerged the Thirteenth, Fourteenth, and
Fifteenth amendments. Also, one of them, Representative
John A. Bingham of Ohio, proclaimed doctrines of equality
which heralded his authorship of the first section of the
Fourteenth Amendment. Under the due process clause of the
Constitution, he argued in Congress, all men are equal under
the law "in respect of those rights which God gives and no
man or state may rightfully take away except, as a forfeiture
for crime . . . those rights common to all men . . . to protect which, not to confer, all good governments are instituted." In the same speech he also referred to the "absolute
equality of all the equal protection of each." [31]

The ideas of protection and equality as elements of the
secular democratic faith were not only a part of the common
political currency of the United States in the formative
period, but they were also important constitutional ingredients. In contrast to the relative paucity of political theory
in the original seven articles of the federal Constitution, the
state constitutions framed and ratified between the Declaration of Independence and the Civil War are rich in the legal
and political ideas of Magna Carta and the social compact.
Most of the state constitutions in this period proclaimed the
doctrine of equality in one of two forms. Some, for example,
asserted that "all men when they form a social compact are
equal in rights" or that all men are born "equally free and
independent"; [32] and some of these confined this generaliza-

---

[31] Quoted in Jacobus tenBroek, *The Antislavery Origins of the Fourteenth
Amendment* (Berkeley and Los Angeles, 1951), 126. Possibly tenBroek over-
emphasizes the contributions of the abolitionists, but his volume contains
very valuable materials.

[32] The collection of state constitutions in Francis N. Thorpe, *The Federal and*

tion to "freemen." [33] Other states made broader claims for equality. Thus the celebrated Massachusetts constitution of 1780 asserted, over the objections of John Adams, that "all men are born free and equal, and have certain natural, essential, and unalienable rights." The Kentucky constitution of 1792 found all men equal when they formed the social compact, but qualified this principle in 1799 by confining it to "all free men." Some of these claims, too, were qualified by other provisions inconsistent with an unlimited equality. Thus the constitution of Oregon of 1857 asserted that all men were equal in rights when they formed the social compact, and in subsequent provisions prohibited the further immigration of free Negroes and mulattoes and excluded Negroes, Chinese, and mulattoes from the suffrage. Nevertheless, a majority of the state constitutions adopted before 1861 contain broad assertions of equality or at least of equality in rights.

Many of the state constitutions, in similar and sometimes identical language, affirmed equality in other terms. Thus the Massachusetts constitution of 1780 declared that government is instituted for the common good "for the protection, safety, prosperity, and happiness of the people, and not for the profit, honor, or private interest of any one man." The Pennsylvania constitution of the same year contained similar provisions. More common, however, was the provision of the Virginia constitution to the effect that no man or set of men is entitled to "exclusive or separate emoluments or privileges from the community, but in consideration of public services." [34]

State Constitutions, Colonial Charters, and other Organic Laws of the States, Territories and Colonies now or heretofore forming the United States of America (7 vols., Washington, 1909), was used for this section. Constitutions of Virginia of 1776; Pennsylvania, 1776; Ohio, 1804; Connecticut, 1818; Illinois, 1818.

[33] Alabama, 1819; Texas, 1845.

[34] This provision was carried over into the Virginia constitutions of 1830 and 1860, and similar provisions were contained in the constitutions of Alabama, 1819; Connecticut, 1818; Michigan, 1835; Mississippi, 1817; North

Equally important is the emphasis which the state constitutions of the late eighteenth and the first half of the nineteenth century place upon protection as one of the common purposes of government. Notice has already been taken of the general recognition of protection as an object of government in the early constitutions of Massachusetts, Pennsylvania, and Virginia. But the constitution of Massachusetts stressed protection in another context. According to Article X, "each individual of the society has a right to be protected by it in the enjoyment of his life, liberty, and property according to standing laws." Similarly, the constitution of Pennsylvania asserted the right of every member of society "to be protected in the enjoyment of life, liberty, and property." [35]

Many of these constitutions also contained with some variations in phraseology sections which were parallels of the fortieth clause of Magna Carta. In Article XI of the Massachusetts constitution is the admonition that "every citizen

---

Carolina, 1776; Texas, 1845. Many of the early state constitutions contained due process or "law of the land" clauses. In the frequently cited and quoted case of *Vanzant* v. *Waddell*, 2 Yerger (Tenn.) 259 (1829), the Tennessee Supreme Court identified the equality and impartiality of the laws with the requirements of the law of the land clause in the state constitution. Judge Jacob Peck asserted in a separate opinion that "a law which is partial in its operation, intended to affect particular individuals alone, or to deprive them of the benefits of the general laws is unwarranted by the constitution and is void. . . ." (269). Judge John Catron, soon to become an Associate Justice of the Supreme Court of the United States, had no doubt that "a partial law, tending to deprive a corporation or an individual of rights of property, or to the equal benefits of the general and public laws of the land is unconstitutional and void. . . ." Citing *Dartmouth College* v. *Woodward*, 4 Wheat. 518 (1819); *Holden* v. *James*, 11 Mass. 396 (1814). In the latter case the Supreme Judicial Court of Massachusetts declared that it was "manifestly contrary to the first principles of civil liberty, natural justice, and the spirit of our constitution and laws that any one citizen should enjoy privileges and advantages which are denied to all others under like circumstances." After citing the above cases, Catron went on to assert that the law of the land clause means "a general and public law, equally binding upon every member of the community." For the juristic connection between liberty and equality, see Edward S. Corwin, *Liberty Against Government* (Baton Rouge, 1948), 75–76, 93–94, 126, 167–68.

[35] See also the constitutions of Vermont of 1777, 1786, and 1793. Vermont had two constitutions before it became a state.

of the commonwealth ought to find a certain remedy by having recourse to the laws, for all injuries or wrongs which he may receive in his person, property or character. He ought to obtain right and justice freely and without being obliged to purchase it; completely, and without any denial; promptly, and without delay; conformably to the laws." Other constitutions provided more simply and more emphatically that the courts "shall" be open and that every person "shall" have a remedy for injuries done him in lands, goods, or person by due course of law and "right and justice administered, without sale, denial, or delay." [36]

One other provision which was incorporated in a few of these constitutions is important because of its form which follows in one clause almost the same phraseology of the equal protection clause. In Article III of the Massachusetts constitution was the provision: "And every denomination of Christians, demeaning themselves peaceably, and as good citizens of the commonwealth, shall be equally under the protection of the law, and no subordination of any one sect or denomination to another shall ever be established by law." [37]

Drafted in the heat of the struggle for national independence or in the mellower light of its afterglow, the Revolutionary constitutions are permeated with the principles of Magna Carta, of the common law as enunciated by its great

[36] Alabama, 1819; Kentucky, 1792; Maryland, 1776; Minnesota, 1858; Mississippi, 1817; New Hampshire, 1784; Ohio, 1804; Pennsylvania, 1790, 1838; Rhode Island, 1842; Tennessee, 1796, 1834; Vermont, 1796, 1834; Wisconsin, 1848.

[37] See the constitutions of Maine, 1819; New Hampshire, 1784. The constitutions of other states prohibited legal preferences of one religion to another, in different phraseology. See, e.g., South Carolina, 1778; Virginia, 1776. Isolated provisions of interest, if not significance, are those of the Ohio constitution of 1804, which provided for the equal participation of the poor in the state schools, academies, colleges, and universities, and that of Wisconsin of 1848, which prohibited any distinction between resident aliens and citizens with respect to the possession, enjoyment, or descent of property.

expositor, Sir William Blackstone, and of the principles of
revolutionary philosophy as refined by Locke and condensed
in the Declaration of Independence. Accordingly, they present
a consistent line of continuity in constitutional development
which culminated in the nationalization of equality and protection in the Fourteenth Amendment. Hence, they are
relevant to the origins and meanings of the equal protection
of the laws. The imitative and repetitious nature of these
constitutions, with their incorporation (in almost identical
language) of the political ideas of the social compact and
Magna Carta, is most important, not because it demonstrates
a rather singular lack of originality, but because it reflects
the consensus and sentiments of America, if not in unanimity,
at least in the loud, clear voice of a majority of legal and
political writers and constitution makers.

At the very least the majority of these constitutions is
dedicated to the following propositions: (1) that all men are
equal in their rights and are equally entitled to the protection
of their enjoyment of the rights of life, liberty, and property;
(2) that the courts shall be open to all for the redress or
prevention of wrongs, and that justice shall be administered
freely without delay or denial; (3) that no man or class of
men has an exclusive right to any special privileges or
emoluments, except as compensation for public services.
Finally, at least three constitutions, in provisions respecting
religion, anticipate the equal protection formula, but express
it in positive terms by guaranteeing that all sects demeaning
themselves peaceably shall be equally under the protection
of the law. Accordingly, the idea of the positive duty of government to afford positive protection of the civil rights to the
individual person by equal laws was a common part of the
American political tradition and its vocabulary long before
the rise of the Abolitionists and, of course, long before
Bingham and his fellow Radicals saw to its inclusion in the
Fourteenth Amendment. In keeping alive the traditions of

equal protection when John C. Calhoun and others were reviving the Aristotelian concept of natural inequality, and in extending the concepts of freedom, equality, and protection to the Negro when it was neither safe nor respectable to do so, the Abolitionists later came to have a pervasive influence on those provisions of the Fourteenth Amendment of enduring importance.

CHAPTER TWO

Reconstruction: The Stormy Debut of the Fourteenth Amendment

CONSTITUTIONAL PRINCIPLES OF equality and protection as evolved from classical political theory, the Roman jurists, the feudal law, the social compact, and the Declaration of Independence played an important role in congressional debates from 1866 through 1875. The debates centered about civil rights legislation, the submission of the Fourteenth Amendment in 1866, and subsequent efforts to implement its provisions by statute, which came to an end in 1875. Conditions in the states comprising the Confederacy stimulated all of the efforts of Congress to strengthen civil rights in this nine-year period and led especially to the enactment of the Civil Rights Act of 1866 and the proposal of the Fourteenth Amendment in 1867. Unchastened by the disaster of military defeat in the war which they helped precipitate, unreconciled to the Thirteenth Amendment, and emboldened by President Johnson's lenient reconstruction policy, southern extremists in a number of states committed a series of blunders which played into the hands of the Radical Republicans and invited the alleged excesses of Reconstruction.

One of these blunders was the enactment of the so-called Black Codes in a number of southern states, which were designed to restore the substance of slavery in different forms by placing serious disabilities upon Negroes with respect to contract, ownership of property, access to courts, and the like. Another blunder, perhaps unavoidable in the chaotic conditions that existed, was the failure to suppress private violence directed largely at Negroes. The result was the enactment in 1866 of the Civil Rights Act [1] and the amendment to the Freedmen's Bureau Act,[2] both of which heralded the coming of more important developments and were of great importance in shaping the congressional attitude on the dual ideas of equality and protection. Of the two acts the Civil Rights Act and the debates on it are the more important in presaging the Fourteenth Amendment.

After making all persons born in the United States and subject to its jurisdiction, excluding Indians not taxed, citizens of the United States, the Act went on to provide that ". . . such citizens, of every race and color, without regard to any previous condition of slavery or involuntary servitude, except as a punishment for crime . . . shall have the same right in every state or territory in the United States, to make and enforce contracts, to sue, be parties, and give evidence, to inherit, purchase, lease, sell, hold, and convey real and personal property, and to full and equal benefit of all laws and proceedings for the security of person and property, as is enjoyed by white citizens, and shall be subject to like pains, and penalties, and to none other, any law, statute, ordinance, regulation, or custom, to the contrary notwithstanding." [3] Given the objective of this provision, the invalidation of the Black Codes and other discriminatory state laws and customs, it is likely that the act did no more than assert the power of Congress to enforce the equality of all citizens before the law, on the assumption that legal dis-

[1] 14 Stat. 27.　　[2] 14 Stat. 173.　　[3] 14 Stat. 27, Sec. 1.

criminations with respect to contract, property, access to the courts, and criminal punishments were a badge of servitude prohibited by the Thirteenth Amendment. However, ten-Broek and others have argued that the act and the debates on it are a reaffirmation, on the basis of Lockean and abolitionist doctrines, of the duty of the federal government to afford positive protection to all citizens in the event of failure of the states to do so either by active discrimination or by withholding adequate protection.[4] The clause, "the same right . . . to full and equal benefit of all laws for the security of person and property," lends some support to this view; but this clause is immediately modified by another, "as is enjoyed by white citizens." The inclusion of custom, however, is most significant, and shows a determination to root out specified racial discriminations founded on custom or unofficial action as well as on law, by which was meant the common law, statutes, court decisions, ordinances, and regulations.

In the Senate the bill was presented by Senator Lyman Trumbull, a moderate by nature, who was thrown among the Radicals by the massive bungling of Andrew Johnson. He reiterated the familiar notions of government by contract, the surrender of some liberties in return for protection of others, and quoted Blackstone on civil liberty and equality. Blackstone had stated with respect to his definition of civil

---

[4] Jacobus tenBroek, *The Antislavery Origins of the Fourteenth Amendment.* There is a prolific literature dealing with the origins and congressional history of the Fourteenth Amendment in addition to the above. Among these are Joseph B. James, *The Framing of the Fourteenth Amendment* (Urbana, Illinois, 1956); Howard Jay Graham, "Our Declaratory Fourteenth Amendment," 7 *Stanford Law Review* 3 (1954); John P. Frank and Robert F. Munro, "The Original Understanding of 'Equal Protection of the Laws,' " 50 *Columbia Law Review* 153 (1950). All of these writers except James emphasize (1) abolitionist theories of due process, privileges and immunities, and equal protection as a guide to the meaning of the first section of the Fourteenth Amendment and (2) their influence on John A. Bingham. An excellent account of the Fourteenth Amendment as a compromise is presented by Alexander M. Bickel, "The Original Understanding and the Segregation Decision," 69 *Harvard Law Review* 1 (1955).

liberty "that the restraints [upon liberty] introduced by the law should be equal to all, or as much so as the nature of things will admit." [5] Therefore, any statute, according to Trumbull, "which is not equal to all, and which deprives any citizen of civil rights which are secured to other citizens, is an unjust encroachment upon his liberty; and is in fact, a badge of servitude which, by the Constitution, is prohibited." He then cited the privileges and immunities clause in Article IV as securing to the citizens of each state "such fundamental rights as belong to every free person." In this context Trumbull referred to the mob which drove Samuel Hoar from South Carolina when he appeared as a lawyer for some free Negro seamen, and the Senator declared that Congress had the power to prevent and punish such interferences as Hoar had encountered.[6]

Trumbull's argument generally asserts a broad power in Congress to enforce the privileges and immunities clause in Article IV and to protect the equal rights of all citizens under the second section of the Thirteenth Amendment. Equality and liberty are inextricably bound together and unequal laws are a deprivation of liberty, a badge of servitude. Moreover, it is the duty of government to afford protection to all, and when the states fail to provide it, as in the Hoar episode, Congress has the power to do so. Other senators argued along similar lines. Democrats and some Republicans narrowly

[5] Sir William Blackstone, *Commentaries on the Laws of England* (London, 1865–1869). The text used is the Chitty edition (Philadelphia, 1832). Trumbull's quotation is taken from footnote 5, I, 90, 91. The thinking of the supporters of the Civil Rights Bill, the Fourteenth Amendment, and subsequent implementing legislation is permeated with Blackstonian concepts. Thus Blackstone asserted that the community must guard the rights of each individual member in return for his submission to the laws of the community (I, 32) and that the "principal aim of society is to protect individuals in the enjoyment of those absolute rights which are vested in them by the immutable laws of nature" (I, 89). For the reciprocal nature of allegiance and protection, see I, 366–71
[6] *Congressional Globe,* 39th Cong., 1st Sess., 474–75. Hereinafter cited as *Cong. Globe.*

construed slavery, challenged the constitutionality of the bill, and raised, among other issues, the specter of mixed schools and miscegenation. Trumbull avowed that the bill would not affect state miscegenation laws, but questions concerning segregated schools were unanswered. Because practices of segregation played a very little role in the debate and were mentioned somewhat fortuitously, the exchange of views between Trumbull and the Democrats is hardly conclusive. Another phase of the Senate debate of more than incidental interest is that some of the advocates of Negro equality were not willing to extend it to the Indians.[7] Finally, Trumbull repeated at various times a distinction between civil rights such as those protected in the bill and political rights like the suffrage, and emphasized that the bill applied only to civil rights.[8]

Representative James F. Wilson of Iowa, who was in charge of the bill in the House, also asserted that the bill did not include such political rights as suffrage or service on juries and that the protection of civil rights did not mean that white and Negro children would have to attend the same schools. He then went on to emphasize the purpose of the bill to remove discriminations by law. Civil rights were identified with the natural rights of man. The guarantee of immunities he regarded as merely securing to citizens of the United States equality in the exemptions of the law. Then he continued: "A colored citizen shall not, because he is colored, be subjected to obligations, duties, pains, and penalties from which other citizens are exempted. Whatever exemptions there may be shall apply to all citizens alike. One race shall not be more favored in this respect than another. One class shall not be required to support alone the burdens which should rest on all classes alike. This is the spirit and scope of the bill, and it goes not one step beyond." [9]

[7] See generally *ibid.*, 476–78, 497–500, 504–50, 573–74.
[8] *Ibid.*, 599.   [9] *Ibid.*, 1117.

Had Wilson stopped here he would have been asserting nothing more than the principle of equality before the law, but he went on to assert the power and duty of the federal government to protect the fundamental rights of life, liberty, and property which existed anterior to the Constitution. He quoted Blackstone and James Kent on the absolute rights of personal security, liberty, and property, and contended that it is the duty of the United States to protect these rights at home as well as abroad because of the mutuality of allegiance and protection. "The entire machinery of government as organized by the Constitution was designed, among other things, to secure a more perfect enjoyment of these rights." [10] M. Russell Thayer of Pennsylvania also spoke of the purpose of the bill to secure the fundamental rights of the freedmen "which constitute the essence of freedom . . . those rights which secure life, liberty, and property, and which make all men equal before the law, as they are equal in the scales of eternal justice and in the eyes of God." [11]

Others emphasized equality and protection in other terms. William Windom of Minnesota said that the bill was designed to give effect to the Declaration of Independence and declared that a "true republic rests upon the absolute equality of rights of the whole people, high and low, rich and poor, white and black." [12] John M. Broomall of Pennsylvania declared that the rights and duties of allegiance are reciprocal and that there can be no allegiance without protection, and Samuel Shellabarger voiced similar sentiments and cited Calhoun as his authority.[13] Thayer contended that the first eleven amendments, instead of being mere limitations on the federal government, were grants of power to it.[14] Finally, William Lawrence of Ohio argued that the obligations of the state and federal governments did not end with the observance of constitutional prohibitions against the abridg-

---

[10] *Ibid.*, 1118–19.   [11] *Ibid.*, 1152.   [12] *Ibid.*, 1159.   [13] *Ibid.*, 1263, 1293–94.   [14] *Ibid.*, 1270, in a colloquy with Michael C. Kerr. See also p. 1152.

ment of fundamental rights, but the means whereby "inherent and indestructible" rights may be protected and enjoyed were equally important. He then proceeded to enumerate two ways whereby a state may deprive citizens of their absolute rights of life, security, liberty, and property: "either by prohibitory laws, or by a failure to protect any one of them." [15]

That the broad assertions of federal power made by the proponents of the Civil Rights Bill raised grave constitutional doubts and rested on serious misconceptions of the Constitution is certain. In identifying the principles of the Declaration of Independence with those of the Constitution, Trumbull and others were but repeating one of the gross historical errors of the Abolitionists. Their understanding of the privileges and immunities clause of Article IV was completely erroneous, and the identification of the first eleven amendments with grants of power was a monstrous absurdity which displayed an ignorance both of constitutional history and of judicial precedents.

[15] *Ibid.*, 1832 ff. It is not surprising that members of Congress with abolitionist backgrounds stressed the duty of all governments to protect persons in the enjoyment of all their rights. The Abolitionists were driven from the South, and because of lack of governmental protection they were subjected to varying degrees of violence in the North, including murder and the destruction of printing presses. Hence they could agree with the Independent Puritans in *The Ancient Bounds* that "civil protection is that which all magistrates owe, whether Christian or not Christian, to all quiet livers within their dominions, whether Christian or not Christian, as being founded upon such politic considerations and conditions (setting aside religion) as, being performed on the subjects part, it cannot with justice be denied them." Woodhouse, *The Ancient Bounds*, 249. The duty of government to protect its citizens in South Carolina as well as in Tripoli was frequently linked to the forced departure of Samuel Hoar from South Carolina. *Supra*, p. 27. *The Nation* put the duty of protection colorfully when it observed editorially that the South would not be fit for restoration to the Union until Wendell Phillips could deliver one of his "most violent and desponding lectures" with no greater danger "than that of being hissed." II, 70 (1866), quoted in James, *The Framing of the Fourteenth Amendment*, 77. Phillips was strong medicine even in New England, where many proper Bostonians shared Judge Hoar's sentiment, "I did not attend Wendell Phillips' funeral, but I approved of it." Quoted in Vernon L. Parrington, *Main Currents in American Thought* (3 vols., New York, 1927–1930), III, 141.

However, the constitutional errors of Trumbull and his followers in no way detract from the force of the underlying assumptions concerning equality and protection and of the essential relationship of the two. On this point both the sponsors and the advocates of the bill could agree. Thus Senator Timothy O. Howe, the Wisconsin Radical, echoing Franklin, could argue that although men are not equal socially, intellectually, and physically, it is the duty of government to make men equal; and, the weaker men are, the more government is "bound to foster and protect them," because the weak are more in need of protection.[16] Senator Edgar Cowan, a conservative from Pennsylvania, opposed the bill, but he equated protection and equality. To him, equality meant that if a man "is assailed by one stronger than himself the Government will protect him to punish the assailant." If a man owes another money, the government will compel the debtor to pay. If a trespasser goes upon his land, "he shall have a remedy to recover it." That, he said, is what is meant "by equality before the law." [17]

The debate on the Freedmen's Bureau Bill added little to what was said during the proceedings on the Civil Rights Bill. It is worthy of attention, however, that when Trumbull gave notice that he was going to introduce it, he used language in speaking of protection which connoted much more than a congressional power to correct discriminatory legislation, namely, the broad power "to secure freedom to all persons within the United States, and protect every individual in the full enjoyment of the rights of persons and property and furnish him with means for their vindication." The enlargement of the powers of the Freedmen's Bureau were necessary, he said, in order to quiet fears that by "local legislation or a prevailing public sentiment" in some states, the Negro should continue to be oppressed and deprived of freedom, and to show to the former slave states that "unless

[16] *Cong. Globe,* 39th Cong., 1st Sess., 438. [17] *Ibid.,* 342.

by local legislation they provide for the real freedom of their former slaves, the Federal Government will, by virtue of its own authority, see that they are fully protected." Trumbull went on to repeat that "any legislation or any public sentiment which deprives any human being in the land of those great rights of liberty will be in defiance of the Constitution; and if the States and local authorities, by legislation or otherwise, deny these rights, it is incumbent on us to see that they are secured." [18] In other words, it is not sufficient that the states treat all persons alike; they must positively protect all alike. Nor does it suffice that the states and their agents or officers observe constitutional guarantees. They must take positive action to provide adequate remedies to secure the rights of liberty against "any prevailing public sentiment." The primary duty to protect civil rights remains with the states; but if they fail to do so, either by imposing discriminations or by failing to provide adequate protection for persons and their rights, Congress has both the power and the duty to act.

Doubts of the constitutionality of the Civil Rights Act were not confined to those unwilling to accept the Negro as an equal. They were shared by men who believed both in the objective of the law and its underlying assumption of the duty of the federal and state governments to provide positive protection to the rights of life, liberty, equality, and property of all men. It is possible, too, that the supporters of the measure who publicly argued for its constitutionality with more confidence than competence were privately troubled by constitutional doubts and fears. Accordingly, a movement was soon launched by Representative Bingham to remove all such doubts by a constitutional amendment. Bingham, it must be emphasized, was an Abolitionist from the Western Reserve, who had been schooled in the social compact doctrines of liberty, equality, and protection which were the com-

[18] *Ibid.,* 77.

mon currency of all Abolitionists. Although Bingham was in favor of the objectives of the Civil Rights Act, he had opposed its passage on grounds of constitutionality. Accordingly, he proceeded to draft one version of a constitutional amendment after another, until he provided the final text of Section 1 of the Fourteenth Amendment minus the citizenship provision in the first sentence.

Actually Bingham's conception of the first section had been anticipated in part by Senator Justin Morrill, a fellow member of the Committee of Fifteen on Reconstruction, when he penned a memorandum to Charles Sumner shortly before the Thirty-ninth Congress convened. Morrill suggested a constitutional amendment which would provide that all citizens of the United States "are equal in their civil rights immunities and privileges and equally entitled to protection in life, liberty, and property." He suggested a provision that no distinction in the right to vote could be made because of color, and that all laws in contravention of these rights would be null and void.[19] Bingham's first draft differed materially both from this proposal and from his final draft, which more nearly resembled Morrill's suggestion.

Among the numerous proposals for securing equal rights and different versions of the same proposal until the final draft of Section 1, the two most important are Bingham's original proposal and the final form. Bingham first proposed, on January 12, 1866, that "Congress shall have power to make all laws necessary and proper to secure to all persons in every State within the Union equal protection in their rights of life, liberty, and property." [20] The implications of such a proposal with regard to congressional power and federalism were shocking to the moderates and even to some Radicals, with the result that it obtained little support. Hence, action upon

[19] Undated letter in 1865 to Charles Sumner, quoted in the excellent study by James, *The Framing of the Fourteenth Amendment*, 30.
[20] Benjamin B. Kendrick (ed.), *The Journal of the Joint Committee of Fifteen on Reconstruction* (New York, 1914), 46.

it was indefinitely postponed by Bingham's own motion on the ground that the proposal passed by the House covered "the whole subject." [21] This proposal, of course, was the first section of the Fourteenth Amendment in its final form, joined by the fifth section which empowered Congress to enforce it. Whether Bingham really believed there were no differences between his first and final proposals, as he seems to have thought when he moved indefinite postponement and when he argued later for the enactment of the Ku Klux Klan Act,[22] is irrelevant except as an example of his obscure thinking. Actually, Bingham's first proposal would have placed on Congress the primary responsibility of enforcing all civil rights so as to bring within federal jurisdiction most of the offenses known to the criminal law, and many civil actions as well. The proposal in its final form left primary responsibility for the protection of civil rights with the states and vested Congress with what subsequently proved to be rather obscure powers.

The desire to retain the basic elements of federalism in the distribution of legislative powers between the nation and the states was coupled with the fear that Bingham's original

[21] *Cong. Globe,* 39th Cong., 1st Sess., 298.

[22] Act of April 20, 1871, 17 Stat. 13. The following passage is typical of Bingham's oratory and thought: "Your constitution provides that no man, no matter what his color, no matter beneath what sky he may have been born, no matter in what disastrous conflict or by what tyrannical hand his liberty may have been cloven down, no matter how poor, no matter how friendless, no matter how ignorant, shall be deprived of life or liberty or property without due process of law—law in its highest sense, that law which is the perfection of human reason, and which is impartial, equal, exact justice; that justice which requires that every man shall have his right; that justice which is the highest duty of nations as it is the imperishable attribute of the God of nations." *Cong. Globe,* 39th Cong., 1st Sess., 1094. These sentiments give added weight to the remarks of Representative Giles W. Hotchkiss of New York, who opposed the resolution as not going far enough. He asserted immediately after Bingham's apostrophe to law and justice: "Constitutions should have their provisions so plain that it will be unnecessary for courts to give construction to them; they should be so plain that the common mind can understand them." *Ibid.,* 1095. The discussion centered about Bingham's initial proposal.

proposal did not place the principles of the Civil Rights Act beyond the power of repeal, and thereby left Negro rights subject to the caprice of fluctuating majorities in Congress. Despite all the carefully designed efforts of the Radicals in Sections 3 and 4 of the amendment to make the country and the South indefinitely safe for the Republican party, an obsessive fear appeared to pervade the utterances of the Radicals in the Thirty-ninth Congress. This fear was that, in the future, Congress would once again be controlled by Democrats, or in the expression of Thad Stevens, "yelling secessionists and hissing copperheads." Accordingly, there was a desire for an amendment that would place the possible abrogation of civil rights beyond the power of southern rebels and their northern allies. Moreover, all, including Bingham, desired to remove constitutional doubts from the Civil Rights Act and comparable legislation which Congress might enact in the future.

Beyond these objectives it is difficult to ascertain from the debates the specific purposes of the first section coupled with the fifth. The greater portion of the debates over the submission of the Fourteenth Amendment centered about the representation and suffrage provisions in Section 2 and the device for disfranchising former Confederates in Section 3. The concern over these two issues reflected both the serious disagreements which existed among the Radical Republicans and also the view of Stevens and others that these two provisions were the heart of the amendment. No serious disagreement existed among the Republicans with respect to Section 1, and many of the Radical leaders, among whom were Stevens and Roscoe Conkling, regarded it as unimportant or, as in Conkling's case, preferred its omission.

Nevertheless, the debates are of some importance in reflecting a state of mind and broad aims as distinguished from specified intentions. A common theme of the discussion by the amendment's supporters was the mutual interdependence of the privileges and immunities, due process, and equal protection clauses, in contrast to the later practice of constitutional lawyers and historians of regarding the clauses as separate and independent. To Bingham, Jacob Howard, and their cohorts the right to be treated equally and to be protected was a privilege and immunity of citizenship, equality was an essential part of liberty, and the right to due process as regards access to the courts and freedom to enter contracts and acquire and dispose of property were parts both of liberty and privileges and immunities of citizenship. Another pervasive theme of the supporters was the reciprocal nature of allegiance and protection. The citizen owed government allegiance and obedience, government owed the citizen protection. Without protection there could be no allegiance. A third theme was the absolute equality of all men before the law, equally and impartially administered. A frequent note, too, was that Section 1 was only declaratory of existing law and that the only change was in Section 5, which provided for congressional implementation and federal enforcement of pre-existing law.

In elaborating on these themes the supporters of the amendment displayed the same confusion in matters of constitutional law that characterized the debate on the Civil Rights Act and the earlier abolitionist arguments, but with all their confusion and redundant and florid language their words are of some significance to the meaning of that harmonious unity which proceeds from the trinity of privileges and immunities, due process of law, and the equal protection of the laws.

The evidence in the debates with respect to the scope of congressional power to secure the rights of persons and to enforce the equal protection clause is inconclusive, and its weight is perhaps on the side of those who would confine congressional power to legislation corrective of unequal state legislation, partial administration of state laws, or failure to enforce them at all. To be sure, Dr. tenBroek and others have demonstrated rather plausibly that the debates reveal a determination to vest Congress with a broader power to enforce the amendment by legislation extending protection to persons in the event of failure of the states to afford it positively and adequately by their own laws. When Bingham introduced his proposed amendment in a positive form, he and others certainly used language that supports this contention. However, the debate in January and February of 1866 is hardly a conclusive guide to the meaning of a substantially different proposal which was debated three and four months later. In the discussion of the final draft Bingham played an active part. In general he was inclined, as were his associates, to use grandiose rhetoric and ambiguous language and to identify aspiration with reality.

In his speech of May 10 Bingham referred to "the equal rights of all the people under the sanctions of inviolable law" and pointed to the necessity of power in Congress to protect "the privileges and immunities of all the citizens of the Republic and the inborn rights of every person within its jurisdiction whenever the same shall be abridged or denied by the unconstitutional acts of any State." He then proceeded to use language that supports a broader congressional power by stating: "No state ever had the right, under the forms of law or otherwise, to deny to any free man the equal protection of the laws or to abridge the privileges or immunities of any citizen of the Republic." However, he soon returned to expressions of a restrictive connotation by saying: "That great want of the citizen and stranger, protection by national law from unconstitutional State enactments, is supplied by the first section of this amendment. That is the extent it hath; no more." [23] To be sure, Bingham was speaking of the first section separately from the fifth, but he was speaking within the context of remarks concerning an alleged

[23] *Cong. Globe,* 39th Cong., 1st Sess., 2542–43.

lack of federal power to protect loyal citizens against South
Carolina's nullification policies.

In closing the debate in the House on May 8, Stevens made
remarks which unequivocally support the restriction of congressional power to the enactment of corrective legislation.
"This Amendment," he declared, "allows Congress to correct
the unjust legislation of the States, so far that the law which
operates upon one man shall operate equally upon all. Whatever law punishes a white man for a crime shall punish the
black man precisely in the same way and to the same degree.
Whatever law protects the white man shall afford 'equal'
protection to the black man. Whatever means of redress is
afforded to one shall be afforded to all." [24] In reporting the
proposed amendment to the Senate, Howard included the
guarantees of the first eight amendments in the privileges and
immunities clause and declared the object of the first section
of the amendment to be "to restrain the power of the States
and compel them at all times to respect these great fundamental guarantees." This was to be done by the fifth section,
which he called "a direct affirmative delegation of power to
Congress to carry out all the principles of all these guarantees,
a power not found in the Constitution." When he came to
the equal protection clause he asserted: "This abolishes all
class legislation in the States and does away with the injustice
of subjecting one caste of persons to a code not applicable to
another. It prohibits the hanging of a black man for a crime
for which the white man is not to be hanged. It protects the
black man in his fundamental rights as a citizen with the
same shield which it throws over the white man." [25] In other
words, equal protection of the laws is equality before the law.

In this brief passage it is ironic that Howard should have
given the widest scope to the privileges and immunities
clause (the most restrictive of the three clauses in that it prohibits only laws abridging the privileges and immunities of

[24] *Ibid.*, 2459.   [25] *Ibid.*, 2766.

citizens) and a narrower scope to the due process and equal protection clauses, which are broader in text and applicable to all persons. However, when he turned to the relation between the first and fifth sections he appeared to give all of the provisions a restrictive interpretation. The amendment with the two sections taken together will "forever disable every one of them [states] from passing laws trenching upon those fundamental rights and privileges which pertain to citizens of the United States, and to all persons who may happen to be within their jurisdiction. It establishes equality before the law, and it gives to the humblest, the poorest, the most despised of the race the same rights and the same protection before the law as it gives the most powerful, the most wealthy, or the most haughty." [26]

Speeches by others display the same ambiguities. John F. Farnsworth's speech in the House affirmed by questions a broad congressional power to protect the rights of life, liberty, and property.[27] In the Senate William D. Stewart, the Nevada moderate, who thought amnesty for Confederates and suffrage for Negroes more important than civil rights bills, stressed the reciprocal nature of allegiance and protection in general terms and the equality of all men before the law.[28] Senator Luke Poland of Vermont used expressions which support a broad congressional power when he spoke of the necessity of removing constitutional doubts from the Civil Rights Act, placing civil rights beyond the power of Congress to repeal, and giving effect to the Declaration of Independence.

Although the debates on the Fourteenth Amendment are important as a discussion of general principles and as one guide among others to its meaning, they are hardly conclusive because of their ambiguity, their inadequate and routine discussion of the first section, and the confusion, not to say ignorance, of some of the speakers, among whom Bingham

[26] *Ibid.*   [27] *Ibid.*, 2539.   [28] *Ibid.*, 2801.

was the most prominent. The confusion and ambiguities of a debate in which some of these equalitarians argued that Chinese could never be equal because they are pagan,[29] and in which extreme opponents like Willard Saulsbury and Garrett Davis in the Senate and Andrew J. Rogers in the House made the most of the *argumentum ad horrendum,* are resolved to some extent when we examine the conditions at which the amendment was directed and its actual text, which is considerably clearer. Such a procedure, too, has the advantage of conforming to the rules of statutory and constitutional interpretation. After all, as Justice Felix Frankfurter has reminded us in another context, what was adopted was the Fourteenth Amendment and not what Thad Stevens, John Bingham, or Jacob Howard said about it.[30]

One purpose of the amendment upon which all historians agree was the validation of the Civil Rights Act of 1866 and its removal from the power of Congress to repeal. The Civil Rights Act asserted a broad power on the part of Congress to protect specified rights not only against unjust legislation but also against prevailing public sentiment and custom. Second, the Civil Rights Act of 1866 and the amendment were aimed at uprooting the Black Codes and forbidding the states in the future to enact unequal laws or to enforce laws otherwise valid with an evil eye and an unequal hand. Third, the members of the Committee of Fifteen were alarmed, or pretended to be, by reports of acts of violence and private outrage against the Negro in the South. The report of Karl Schurz and testimony taken before the Committee contained evi-

---

[29] Representative William Higby, a Radical from California, was extremely anti-Chinese. According to him, the Chinese were "a pagan race" of no virtue and incapable of citizenship. By contrast, the Negro was a native and not a pagan. *Ibid.,* 1056. Although Higby's views tended to be extreme, the ideals of other Radical equalitarians did not extend to Indians (*supra,* note 7), to women, or, in some instances, to aliens. Such prejudices, however, support the conclusion that the Radical Republicans intended to make the Negro the absolute equal of the white before the law.

[30] *Adamson* v. *California,* 332 U.S. 46 (1947).

dence of murders, beatings, and other atrocities against Negroes and northerners in the South. That such reports may have been exaggerated is irrelevant in a sordid period where exaggeration was common on both sides and truth often a stranger to each. Some of the violence did occur. It would be astounding, therefore, if the amendment had not been directed at empowering Congress to protect the lives and rights of persons when the states persistently showed either unwillingness or impotence to do so.

More important are the words of the text of the first and fifth sections. The prohibition that "no State shall make or enforce any law which shall abridge the privileges or immunities of citizens of the United States," is fully clear save for the content of privileges and immunities. The prohibition is that the states, by legislation or by the common law, by adjudication or by execution, cannot abridge the privileges or immunities of citizenship. This prohibition is directed at the making or enforcing of such laws. Although in a sense the content of the phrase privileges or immunities of citizens was vague in 1866, there was the oft-quoted and cited opinion of Justice Bushrod Washington in *Corfield* v. *Coryell*,[31] in which he defined privileges or immunities of state citizenship as those "which are, in their nature, fundamental; which belong of right to the citizens of all free governments." Justice Washington enumerated among others the following rights as examples of what are fundamental: "Protection by the Government; the enjoyment of life and liberty, with the right to acquire and possess property of every kind, and to pursue and obtain happiness and safety; subject nevertheless to such restraints as the Government may justly prescribe for the general good of the whole." He also mentioned the right of a citizen of one state to pass through and reside in another for purposes of earning a livelihood, to claim the right of habeas corpus, to have access to the courts

[31] 6 Fed. Cas. No. 3230 (1823).

of the state, and to be exempt from higher taxes and other impositions than are paid by other citizens of the state.

The wording of the due process clause is substantially different, and the prohibition is "nor shall any state deprive any person of life, liberty or property without due process of law." Here the prohibition has become broader and is not confined to the making or enforcement of some law. The various meanings which may be attributed to this clause have long been the subject of controversy and interpretation, but one need only mention here one of the interpretations of the Supreme Court, to the effect that due process requires a minimum of protection by the states of life, liberty, and property. The last clause, "nor deny to any person within its jurisdiction the equal protection of the laws," has for its subject any state, not any law. Hence the states, by law or otherwise, cannot deny equal protection of the laws. None has ever disputed the proposition that the clause establishes equality before the law and requires the states to treat all persons equally. However, to confine the meaning of equal protection to equality before the law is to overlook the meaning of "deny" and the inclusion of "protection."

The clause does more, therefore, than condemn unequal state laws or the unequal enforcement of equal laws; it requires the states to provide or afford equal protection of the laws. Neither a strenuous exercise in philology nor an examination of usage in 1866 is required to define the word "deny." It meant then within the context of the amendment what it meant long before and continues to mean, to refuse to grant, to withhold, to forbid access to, to refrain from giving some claim, right, or favor. Accordingly, the prohibition against the denial of equal protection of the laws is the same thing as a positive requirement which could read, "Every state shall afford, or furnish, every person within its jurisdiction the equal protection of the laws."

Why, then, was the clause put in the negative? One answer

is that it was a fairly common practice to express constitutional limitations, especially in the federal constitution, negatively. A second is that when the clause is read with the fifth section empowering Congress to enforce the provisions of the amendment by appropriate legislation, it is considerably stronger. Laws that are unequal on their face or that are administered unequally are automatically void, so that the condemnation of unequal laws is self-executing without corrective legislation. Moreover, the failure of a state to provide protection, either by neglecting to enact adequate laws or to enforce those already enacted, is subject to the corrective power of Congress to supply the protection which the states cannot or will not supply. Such a construction is consistent not only with the text of the amendment, but also with the development of constitutional theory through Magna Carta, Locke, and the American Revolution, and later confirmed by numerous state constitutions.

Such a construction also makes meaningful the fifth section. If the amendment merely means, as the Supreme Court has generally held, that no state shall make or enforce any unequal laws, the word protection is not only eliminated by construction, but Congress is left with little or nothing to do by appropriate legislation. To say that the fifth section was designed merely to empower Congress to vest jurisdiction in the federal courts to hear cases involving state action contrary to equal protection, as Senator Allen G. Thurman of Ohio later argued, is to ignore the power that Congress already possessed under the judicial article and the necessary and proper clause. The only construction that makes the first and fifth sections of the amendment meaningful is that the states have a constitutional duty to afford protection equally to all persons, and that if they fail in this primary responsibility Congress has the secondary power to supply the deficiency.

Another reason for putting the clause in the negative was

the desire of many members of Congress to disturb as little as possible the basic features of federalism when they were simultaneously conferring new powers upon the national government and placing new limitations upon the states. Bingham's original formula would have placed on Congress the primary responsibility of protecting the rights of persons; the amendment as adopted left this responsibility with the states, but empowered Congress to correct state acts of omission and commission by supplying positive protection. It is altogether possible, too, that the amendment was poorly drafted. Certainly it was, if it conforms to the extravagant claims made for it by some of its original advocates and opponents. When we return to the text one other question remains with respect to the equal protection to which all persons are entitled—equal protection of what? Of the laws, but what laws? When the three clauses are read together as they ought to be, it is equal protection by equal laws pertaining to the rights of life, liberty, property, and the privileges and immunities of citizenship. Or, as expressed by Justice Washington, those rights which are by their nature fundamental and belong as of right to citizens of all free governments.

Many of these questions are covered in detail by the constitutional debate provoked in the House of Representatives by the introduction of the Ku Klux Klan Bill. In its original form the bill imposed civil liability for damages in the federal courts on all persons, official or private, who should deprive any person within the jurisdiction of the states of his constitutional rights. It also authorized the President to suppress insurrections or conspiracies to deprive any person or class of the privileges and immunities secured by the bill as a denial of the equal protection of the laws, whenever the state authorities were unable or unwilling to suppress them. Another section authorized the President to suspend the writ of habeas corpus and to proclaim martial law in situations where armed combinations were able to defy the authority of the state, or when the constituted state authorities should be accomplices with them and convictions of offenders were impracticable.

Three major views of the scope of congressional power under the Fourteenth Amendment emerged during the long debate. The first view embraced a construction of the amendment which sustained almost unlimited congressional power to protect constitutional rights against both official and private action, to the point of displacing state authority altogether without awaiting abridgments of constitutional rights. A second and more moderate view also assumed that Congress had the responsibility and the power to protect constitutional rights in the event of failure of the states to do so, but only after the states had failed or refused to do their duty. A third view was advanced by a minority consisting almost exclusively of Democrats, who argued that congressional power was limited to the elimination of unequal laws and the correction of official or state action alone, so that an equal denial of all protection was no violation of the amendment.

The speech of the ubiquitous Bingham is illustrative of the arguments of the first group. Boasting that he had the honor to add the first section "as it now stands letter for letter, and syllable for syllable" except the provision on citizenship, Bingham in effect argued that there was no difference in congressional power between that contemplated in his original positive proposal and that in the negative version ultimately adopted. He quoted the fortieth clause of Magna Carta: "We will sell to no man, we will not deny or delay to any man right or justice," and argued that the words of the amendment were as comprehensive as those of Magna Carta. He attributed his change from a positive to a negative proposal to a re-examination of *Barron* v. *Baltimore*,[32] in which Chief Justice Marshall indicated that if the framers of the first

[32] 7 Pet. 243 (1833).

eight amendments to the Constitution had intended to limit
the states, they would have followed the language of the
original Constitution in those clauses which imposed restrictions on the states. That, Bingham said, is what he did.

He then adduced a new argument to the effect that the
differences between the privileges of national and state citizenship were chiefly defined in the first eight amendments.
Prior to the Fourteenth Amendment, he argued, a state could
deny a citizen the right of trial by jury, punish a man for giving food and shelter to a fugitive slave, or for teaching an
Indian to read the New Testament. With the amendment the
states could do none of these things, and Congress had the
power to provide that no man shall be tried in state courts
without an impartial jury, that no property can be taken by
a state without payment of just compensation, and it could
declare that no state shall make or enforce any law abridging
freedom of speech or the press, or the right of peaceable assembly. These, he affirmed, "are of the rights of citizens of
the United States defined in the Constitution and guarantied
by the fourteenth amendment, and to enforce which Congress is thereby expressly empowered." [33]

In a different way Aaron F. Perry of Ohio argued that it
was the duty of the states to afford positive protection equally
to all persons. The states could neither abridge nor permit
to be abridged those rights, deny nor fail to afford the equal
protection of the laws. Hence, when the states failed to provide protection, Congress might do so.[34] A similar argument
was made by Shellabarger, a member of the Thirty-ninth
Congress and supporter of the Fourteenth Amendment when
it was under consideration.[35] Representative George F. Hoar
made a similar argument and contended that unless more
than affirmative action by the states were required, the fifth
section would have been unnecessary. He also listed the

[33] *Cong. Globe,* 42d Cong., 1st Sess., append., 85.
[34] *Ibid.,* append., 80.   [35] *Ibid.,* append., 69.

"right to receive a full, free ample education from the Government" as one of the civil rights protected by the amendment.[36] The bill as originally drafted and the somewhat unhistorical claims for congressional power made by Bingham evoked disagreement from Farnsworth and James A. Garfield, whose radicalism in the Thirty-ninth Congress was beyond question. The former reviewed the proceedings in the Thirty-ninth Congress and quoted both Bingham and Stevens in support of his contention that the equal protection clause was directed against unequal state laws as distinguished from the broader power contemplated for Congress under Bingham's original proposal.[37]

The most significant speech of the debate was made by Garfield. He reviewed fully the legislative history of the first section and argued that Bingham's original proposal failed because it proposed such a radical change in the Constitution that it was supported neither by leading Republicans nor by a congressional majority of two-thirds.[38] Accordingly, Garfield contended that the first section operated directly on the states, in contrast to Bingham's first plan which vested Congress with a plenary power to act on persons exclusive of state power. The equal protection clause was, therefore, a restriction on state governments, restraining them "from making or enforcing laws which are not on their face and in their provisions of equal application to all the citizens of the State." The first section, he continued, does not require the laws to be perfect. "They may be unwise, injudicious, even unjust; but they must be equal in their provisions, like the air of heaven, covering all and resting upon all with equal weight." However, the "laws must not only be equal on their face, but they must be so administered that equal protection under them shall not be denied to any class of citizens either by the courts or the executive officers of the State." Had

[36] *Ibid.*, 334–35.   [37] *Ibid.*, append., 115–17.
[38] *Ibid.*, 1000; *ibid.*, append., 150.

Garfield stopped here, his position would have been identical with that of Farnsworth and similar to that of the Democrats, but he went on to express his thought that although it might be pressing the words beyond their natural limits, the provision "that the States shall not 'deny the equal protection of the laws' implies that they shall afford equal protection."

He then addressed his remarks to specific means for enforcing the amendment. In times of peace appeals from state to federal courts would suffice. Otherwise, Congress had authority to provide "for the punishment of all persons, official or private, who shall invade these rights, and who by violence, threats, or intimidation shall deprive any citizen of their fullest enjoyment." The major complaint giving rise to the bill, he said, was not that the laws were unjust or unequal, but even when equal on their face, "by a systematic maladministration of them, or a neglect or refusal to enforce their provisions, a portion of the people are denied equal protection under them." Therefore, in such a situation the equal protection clause empowers Congress to act and "provide for doing justice to those persons who are thus denied equal protection." Accordingly, he would support the bill with amendments which would not assert the power of Congress "to take jurisdiction of the subject until such denial be clearly made, and shall not in any way assume the original jurisdiction of the rights of private persons and of property within the States." [39]

It remained for the Democrats and a few conservative Republicans to argue that the first section of the amendment was self-executing or operative of its own force and that the power of Congress was limited to vesting jurisdiction in the federal courts to apply its terms. Thus Representative James

---

[39] *Ibid.*, append., 153. Jeremiah Wilson of Indiana argued that the states must afford equal protection and that in providing remedies in the event of their failure to do so, Congress is "the exclusive judge," both of the necessity of remedies and what they shall be. *Ibid.*, 483. Representative Poland was closer to Garfield's view. *Ibid.*, 514.

G. Blair of Missouri, a so-called liberal Republican, protested that the restraints of the amendment were directed only to the action of a state in its corporate capacity, and Congress had no power to control the acts of private persons in the event of failure of the state to provide positive protection. He regarded the bill as designed for federal absorption of all governmental power. George W. Morgan, Democrat from Ohio, argued that the only power conferred was that to provide for access to the courts for the redress of wrongs committed in violation of the amendment,[40] and other Democrats, like Michael C. Kerr of Indiana and John B. Storm of Pennsylvania, advanced the original idea of the Radicals that the amendment was only declaratory of existing law, to conclude that it conferred no new powers on the national government.[41]

In the Senate the debate on the Ku Klux Bill was much less extensive, not because of any inhibitions in that body against talking, but because its time had been spent in debating John Sherman's resolution to direct the Committee on the Judiciary to bring in a bill to suppress disorders in the South. This resolution was made in the face of obstruction by chairman Senator Trumball, who had broken with the Radicals and opposed their legislative proposals. The speeches of the bill's supporters add little to what had been said in the House concerning the positive duty of the states to afford equal protection and the power of Congress to act directly on private persons when the states failed in their duty, so that the speeches of Republicans like Oliver H. P. T. Morton, John Pool, and Matt H. Carpenter need not be reviewed. It is of some significance that George F. Edmunds of Vermont, perhaps the best constitutional lawyer in Congress and one of the best in the country, closed the debate

---

[40] *Ibid.,* 331.
[41] *Ibid.,* 48–49, append., 87. See also the speech of Samuel S. Cox, a Democrat from New York, *Ibid.,* 455.

in support of the bill by emphasizing the positive duty of the states to afford protection. Though negative in form, the equal protection clause was affirmative in nature and "grants an absolute right" which Edmunds traced to the origins of liberty in Anglo-Saxon times and to the fortieth clause of Magna Carta.[42]

The supporters of the bill in the Senate had the votes to assure passage and, like a lover wooing his mistress, were in little mood to tarry. Much of the debate, therefore, was consumed by the opposition. Senator Trumbull, in opposing the bill, contended that the Fourteenth Amendment added nothing new to the powers of Congress under the Thirteenth Amendment and, like the Civil Rights Act of 1866, was directed at uprooting unequal legislation like the Black Codes. Democrats such as Thurman, John P. Stockton, Eli Saulsbury, Francis P. Blair, Jr., Thomas F. Bayard, and Garrett Davis argued that the first section did no more than make the Negro a citizen and protect him against discrimination by state or official action under unequal laws, statutory or common. Although Saulsbury conceded the power of Congress to act in the actual presence of "unjust discrimination . . . in the protection given by the laws of a State," Congress lacked a general power to interfere in state affairs and could intervene only when protection was unequal. Hence, the equal withholding of protection from all would not in his view violate the equal protection clause.[43] Senator Blair went so far as to argue that the fifth section did not apply to the first section.[44]

Another contemporaneous interpretation by Congress of the equal protection clause is the Civil Rights Act of 1875.[45] This act was designed to secure to all persons in the jurisdiction of the United States "the full and equal enjoyment

[42] *Ibid.*, 697.
[43] *Ibid.*, 600. See also pp. 573, 575–78, and append., 223, 231, 243.
[44] *Ibid.*, append., 231.   [45] 18 Stat. 335.

of the accommodations, facilities, and privileges of inns, public conveyances, . . . theaters, and other places of public amusement, subject only to the conditions and limitations established by law, and applicable alike to citizens of every race and color, regardless of any previous condition of servitude," and to prohibit the disqualification of any person for jury or grand jury service on account of race, color, or previous condition of servitude.

This legislation was an outgrowth of bills persistently introduced in the Senate by Charles Sumner from 1872 until his death in 1874, and by others in the House. Sumner's bills and similar proposals in the House originally included prohibitions of segregation by public and private schools, churches, and cemeteries. Sumner's bill was effectively kept from the floor of the Senate for two years by the obstinacy of Trumbull, who, as chairman of the Committee on the Judiciary, matched Sumner's persistence by refusing to report the bill. Finally, when it did pass in the Senate, it died in the House. Bills originally introduced in the House fared little better. All, however, resulted in sporadic debates which reaffirmed the power of Congress asserted in 1866, 1870, and 1871 to eliminate inequalities and to provide protection when the states failed in their duty. There is, however, in these debates a somewhat greater emphasis on absolute equality before the law and on segregation as a form of discrimination than was present in the debate of 1871, where the discussion centered more about protection and the duty of the states and the power of Congress to provide it. Thus the bill was designed, according to Sumner, "so that hereafter in all our legislation there shall be no such word as 'black' or 'white,' but that one shall speak only of citizens and of men." [46] Frederick T. Frelinghuysen argued that the equal protection guarantee, reinforced by the privileges and immunities clause, extended to all discriminations because of

[46] 2 *Congressional Record*, 948. Hereinafter cited as *Cong. Rec.*

race "in favor of perfect equality before the law." [47] Earlier
Sumner, in a more realistic mood than usual, had argued that
inns, schools, theaters, and transportation facilities as creatures of the law possessed something of a franchise and were
endowed with a public character because of their special
privileges. Hence they were subject to special responsibilities.

The opposition, led by Senator Thurman of Ohio, followed the main line of constitutional reasoning of the earlier
debate by confining the application of the amendment to
official or state action and constricting the power of Congress
to corrective legislation of unequal state laws. The opposition
also contended that the bill was aimed at social equality, that
Negroes preferred separate schools, and that a requirement
for mixed schools would destroy public education in the
South, but some of these arguments were directed at policy
and not power. Finally, there was the argument advanced by
Thurman that if Congress could obliterate discrimination
based on race, it could outlaw discrimination because of sex
or any other reason. In his view, therefore, the power of Congress was confined to legislation vesting jurisdiction in the
federal courts to hear cases involving state laws as invalid discriminations.[48]

The policy arguments of the bill's opponents were more
effective than their constitutional arguments, so that prohibitions against segregation by schools, churches, and cemeteries were dropped from the bill, not because of doubts concerning constitutionality, but for reasons of policy generally
and political strategy in particular.

The significance of the Ku Klux Act,[49] the Civil Rights
Act of 1875, and the debates on them as evidences of
the meaning of the Fourteenth Amendment is difficult to
estimate. However, as contemporaneous expositions of the

[47] *Ibid.*, 3554.
[48] *Ibid.*, 4084, 4089, 4115; 43d Cong., 2d Sess., 3 *Cong. Rec.* 1791 ff. See also
   Thurman's speech in the 42d Cong., 2d Sess., *Cong. Globe*, append., 29.
[49] 17 Stat. 13.

amendment by men, some of whom were members of the Thirty-ninth Congress and of the Committee of Fifteen on Reconstruction, they are entitled to serious consideration as guides to interpretation. They establish a number of facts or principles beyond controversy. First, despite differences of opinion concerning the scope of congressional power under the amendment, a majority of the members of the Thirty-ninth, Forty-second, and Forty-third Congresses, some of whom were members of all three and of the Committee of Fifteen on Reconstruction, believed that the equal protection clause did more than condemn official or state action. They believed that it vested Congress at the very least with a primary power to set aside unequal state laws and a secondary power to afford protection to all persons in their enjoyment of constitutional rights when the states failed in their primary responsibility to do so either by neglecting to enact laws or by refusal or impotence to enforce them. In this respect Garfield's speech on the Ku Klux Bill is most persuasive. He had supported the Civil Rights and Freedmen's Bureau bills and the proposal for the Fourteenth Amendment in the Thirty-ninth Congress. He displayed, as did many other supporters of these proposals, a solicitude for preserving federalism in its essential features. His interpretation of the first and fifth sections is the only interpretation that is compatible with the maintenance of federalism and simultaneously gives meaning to the equal protection clause and the fifth section vesting power in Congress to enforce the amendment.

Second, a majority of the members of these Congresses regarded Congress as the primary organ for the implementation of the guarantees of privileges and immunities, due process, and equal protection. This does not mean that the Radical Republicans intended to preclude judicial action to apply provisions condemning discrimination by their own force; they did not. However, the Radicals did not trust the judiciary in general and the Supreme Court in particular, either before or after the passage of the resolution submitting the proposed amendment to the states. Former Abolitionists had not forgiven the Court for its decision in the Dred Scott case [50] or for Chief Justice Roger B. Taney's circuit court opinion in *Ex parte Merryman*.[51] The hostility of Radicals to the Court was intensified by Chief Justice Salmon P. Chase's refusal to hold circuit court in states under martial law, thereby preventing the trial of Jefferson Davis, and the fears that their reconstruction policies would be invalidated.

After the submission of the proposed amendment, congressional Radicals and their journalistic allies were successively infuriated by the decision in *Ex parte Milligan*,[52] which rescued a "Copperhead" from a well-deserved hanging by the Court's temerity in merely hearing without deciding a case challenging the validity of the Reconstruction Act,[53] the Court's invalidation of the test oath in the Garland [54] and Cummings [55] cases, the Court's initial assumption of jurisdiction in the McCardle case,[56] and its narrow construction of the Fourteenth Amendment in the Slaughterhouse Cases.[57] All of these actions hit tender spots, and the Garland and Cummings decisions and the Slaughterhouse Cases had deprived the Radicals of the fruits of their military and political victories. The Court was condemned with all the invective which is a part of the treasure of the English language, in expressions that were not to have a parallel until southerners enraged by the Segregation Cases [58] in 1954 adopted the

---

[50] *Dred Scott* v. *Sandford*, 19 How. 393. (1857).
[51] 17 Fed. Cas. No. 9487 (1861).
[52] 4 Wall. 2 (1866). Decided soon after submission of the Fourteenth Amendment.
[53] *Mississippi* v. *Johnson*, 4 Wall. 475 (1867); *Georgia* v. *Stanton*, 6 Wall. 50 (1868).
[54] *Ex parte Garland*, 4 Wall. 333 (1867).
[55] *Cummings* v. *Missouri*, 4 Wall. 277 (1867).
[56] *Ex parte McCardle*, 7 Wall. 506 (1869).   [57] 16 Wall. 36 (1873).
[58] *Brown* v. *Topeka Board of Education*, 347 U.S. 483 (1954).

language and the tactics of their ancestors' enemies. The Court was denounced as a refuge for treason and a usurper, basing its opinions on policy and not law, and numerous bills, two of which passed, were introduced to curtail and even abolish the appellate jurisdiction of the Court and to diminish its membership. On one occasion the irrepressible Bingham even suggested the possibility of reducing the number of justices to three, and appeared generous in stopping there.[59]

A second factor in Radical attitudes toward judicial enforcement is that evidence presented before the Committee of Fifteen and the Ku Klux Committee, regardless of possible exaggerations, confirmed a belief on the part of the Radicals that violence and threats of violence, intimidation, and social and economic pressure against or upon the Negro would prevent him from asserting his rights in the courts. They were, therefore, devising remedies of a governmental nature as a part of the criminal law, which would apply despite the fear, ignorance, indifference, or impotence of Negroes to go into the federal courts to protect their rights.

A third principle that emerges from these debates is that the equal protection clause means absolute or perfect equality before the law and condemns every discrimination perpetrated by unequal laws, partial or maladministration of existing laws by courts or executives, or discriminations by quasi-public businesses or agencies possessing a peculiar status or privilege under the law, such as inns, public conveyances, and the like. With respect to whether the equal protection clause of its own force condemned antimiscegenation laws and segre-

[59] For Radical attacks on the Court, see Charles Warren, *The Supreme Court in United States History* (3 vols., Boston, 1924), III, 91, 143–56, 167–76, 196–97. For the attacks in the House see *Cong. Globe*, 40th Cong., 2d Sess., 478 ff.; in the Senate, *ibid.*, 1859, 1881 ff. The decisions of the Supreme Court following congressional submission of the Fourteenth Amendment, by making real the fearful thinking of the Radicals with respect to the judicial fate of Reconstruction, obviously intensified their earlier belief that the Court could not be trusted and that Congress was the major organ for implementing the amendment.

gation laws and customs, the evidence is inconclusive. That Congress sought to condemn by law some form of segregation in 1875 is a partial argument that it did not. However, the answer to this argument is that judicial remedies alone were regarded as inadequate to prevent discrimination. More important is the failure of Congress to condemn segregation in the schools of the District of Columbia and the neglect of many of the states which ratified the amendment to establish mixed schools. It is quite possible that the amendment of its own force condemned segregation only when it worked a discrimination because of race, which, as a matter of fact, it always has done.

If these conclusions be correct, the Supreme Court has emasculated the first and fifth sections of the Fourteenth Amendment by confining the prohibitions of due process and equal protection to state or official action and by limiting congressional power to the enactment of legislation corrective of official discriminatory actions. Such an interpretation, then, is a departure from and a distortion of the Constitution that has few parallels in American constitutional development, and one of these is the distortion of the due process and equal protection clauses so as to protect property and freedom of contract against state economic regulation.

CHAPTER THREE

Equal Protection as a Shield for Economic and Other Interests

JUSTICE SAMUEL F. MILLER INTER-preted history correctly in the Slaughterhouse Cases [1] when he found "the one pervading purpose" of the Civil War amendments to be "the freedom of the slave race" and "the protection of the newly made freemen and citizen from the oppressions of those who had formerly exercised dominion over him." [2] To be sure, he hastily added, also correctly, this did not mean that no one except the Negro shared in this protection, because, second to the Negro, the framers of the Fourteenth Amendment had in mind the protection of the much hated, frequently abused, and sometimes maligned carpetbagger.

However, Justice Miller was much better as a historian than as a prophet, because when he disposed of the equal protection clause in two brief paragraphs, he doubted very much that any action not discriminating against Negroes as a class and because of their race "would ever come within the purview of this provision." [3] Twelve years later cases started coming to the Court involving economic interests and the

[1] 16 Wall. 36 (1873).   [2] *Ibid.*, 71.   [3] *Ibid.*, 81.

power of the states to classify business and property for purposes of regulation and taxation, and thereafter they came
with increasing frequency. In 1886 the Court unanimously
held with Justice Miller's silent concurrence that the equal
protection clause applied to corporations, and thereby extended judicial hospitality to what were soon to be frequent
visitors, in a casual announcement by Chief Justice Morrison
R. Waite.[4]

Throughout its constitutional history the equal protection
clause has undergone alternative periods of simultaneous
judicial expansion and contraction. From 1873, when cases
involving economic interests alone began coming to the
Court, until 1937 there was a judicial expansion of the clause
to protect interests of business and property against discriminatory state action. Simultaneously, the Court con-
tracted the privileges and immunities clause and a short time
later considerably restricted the scope of equal protection
with respect to discriminations based upon race. Then in
1937 it began to restrict equal protection as a shield of economic interests and to continue an expansion of the clause
begun two years earlier in the area of racial discrimination.
Such a process resulted in substantial changes in judicial
interpretation, but without any significant number of reversals of earlier precedents, although there were some which
will be noted subsequently. The varying and occasionally
conflicting interpretations in turn usually had some justification in terms of the specific text of the amendment as distin-

[4] *County of Santa Clara* v. *Southern Pacific R. Co.*, 118 U.S. 394 (1886). Chief
Justice Waite announced tersely at the hearing: "The Court does not wish to
hear argument on the question whether the provision in the Fourteenth
Amendment to the Constitution, which forbids a State to deny to any person within its jurisdiction the equal protection of the laws, applies to these
Corporations. We are all of the opinion that it does." The meticulous may
regard as most casual this unusual method of disposing of an important
constitutional issue (not before the Court and without argument in the in-
stant case), independently of the Court's opinion written by Justice Harlan.
The decision invalidated assessments on portions of railroad property, without reaching any constitutional issue.

guished from some putative intent of its framers, even though it can be argued that different interpretations, except those enunciating equality before the law, would have been closer both to the text of the amendment and to its theoretical and legal antecedents.

Even so, it is paradoxical that cases involving economic interests having nothing to do with racial or personal discrimination far outnumber all others combined. In the course of making this study 554 decisions of the Supreme Court in which the equal protection clause was invoked and passed upon have been examined. No claim is made that these completely exhaust the cases involving equal protection, but they account for most of them and include all into which discrimination entered because of race, nationality, or color. Of these, 426, or 76.9 per cent, dealt with legislation affecting economic interests. In turn, 255 of these decisions dealt with regulation, and 171 with taxation. State laws allegedly imposing racial discrimination or acts of Congress designed to eliminate it were involved in 78 cases, or in only 14.2 per cent of the total. Seven cases involved discrimination against women, nine were concerned with political discriminations by way of malapportionment of representation and the like, and one with religious discrimination against the Jehovah's Witnesses and their right to make nuisances of themselves in a public park. The remaining 33 had to do with miscellaneous statutes involving criminal procedure, laws applicable to cities on the basis of size, and matters equally unexciting.

The relative paucity of cases relating to racial discrimination can be attributed to a number of factors. Members of some minority groups, particularly Negroes, have been generally poor and uneducated, and poverty and ignorance are great deterrents to litigation. Some, too, are indifferent. Social pressure, threats of economic reprisal, intimidation, and fear have also played a part at different times and in varying degrees in discouraging legal protests against racial discrimination. In this respect we need merely to note that as Negroes have risen economically and educationally, suits challenging discrimination have become more frequent. Likewise, organizations not only of Negroes but of other minority groups have arisen to provide financial support to individual persons to pay the costs of litigation in criminal and civil proceedings.

The numbers of cases, however, are insignificant in themselves because in a large majority of the cases involving classification for purposes of regulation, equal protection was either subsidiary to due process or it was invoked to protect very trivial interests. Although some of these cases are important, many of them do little more than display the Court's patience in dealing with trivia or the highly developed litigious instincts of Homo Americanus. However, some of these yield important principles. Many display, too, the nature of equal protection as a refuge for desperate counsel making one last futile effort in behalf of a losing issue.[5] The 171 cases dealing with classification of property for taxation have their share of issues in which the majestic grandeur of judicial review enshrouds the insignificant, but they are on the whole more important because of their subject matter, the economic interests involved, and the fact that equal protection is frequently the sole or major issue, with due process and obstructions to interstate commerce as subsidiary issues. Not all of the 78 cases dealing with racial discrimination are of cosmic

---

[5] Justice Holmes once said of appeals to the equal protection clause: "It is the usual last resort of constitutional arguments to point out shortcomings of this sort." *Buck* v. *Bell*, 274 U.S. 200, 208 (1927). Here, one argument against the validity of Virginia's compulsory sterilization law applicable to mental defectives in state institutions was that the statute applied only to the few mentally deficient persons confined to state institutions and not to the multitudes outside. Justice Holmes did not comment on this unflattering view of the human race, but did repeat the principle that "the law does all that is needed when it does all that it can" and seeks "to bring within the lines all similarly situated so far and so fast as its means allow." He then concluded that insofar as the release of sterilized mental defectives would open the asylum to those outside, equality would be more nearly attained.

importance, by any means, but some of them are very significant, and as a whole their numbers belie their relative importance. The remaining categories, with some exceptions,
are characterized by their insignificance or rarity.

Although the cases affecting business regulation are the
most numerous, they do admit of generalization and show
on the whole a stability in terms of following precedent that
should satisfy all but the most devoted supporters of *stare
decisis*. One of the earliest of these cases, *Barbier* v. *Connolly*,[6]
continues to be a leading case. It dealt with a rather commonplace ordinance of the city and county of San Francisco requiring separate permits from the health officer and fire
wardens to operate laundries or washhouses within designated city and county limits, and authorizing the health and
fire departments to impose regulations on laundries. A unanimous Court, speaking by the extreme individualist, Justice
Stephen J. Field, sustained the ordinance as a valid exercise
of the police power and propounded important principles of
constitutional interpretation. No invidious distinction was
found, and all persons engaged in the same business were
treated alike. The Fourteenth Amendment, according to the
Court, meant that ". . . equal protection and security should
be given to all under like circumstances in the enjoyment of
their personal and civil rights, that all persons should be
equally entitled to pursue their happiness and acquire and
enjoy property; that they should have like access to the courts
of the country for the protection of their persons and property, the prevention and redress of wrongs, and the enforcement of contracts; that no impediment should be interposed
to the pursuits of anyone except as applied to the same pursuits by others under like circumstances; that no greater
burdens should be laid upon one than are laid upon others
in the same calling and condition, and that in the administration of criminal justice no different or higher punishment

[6] 113 U.S. 27 (1885).

should be imposed upon one than such as is prescribed for all like offenses." However, the amendment was not designed to interfere with the power of the state "to prescribe regulations to promote the health, peace, morals, education and good order of the people, and to legislate so as to increase the industries of the state, to develop its resources and add to its wealth and prosperity." Legislation of a special character and special burdens are often necessary for drainage or irrigation districts, water supply, fire prevention, street cleaning, and the maintenance of parks. Though special in character, such distinctions are valid so long as they apply alike to "all persons and property under the same circumstances and conditions." Justice Field concluded his brief discourse on classification by saying: "Class legislation, discriminating against some and favoring others, is prohibited; but legislation which, in carrying out a public purpose, is limited in its application, if within the sphere of its operation it affects alike all persons similarly situated, is not within the Amendment." [7]

By 1901 the Court had elaborated rules for resolving conflicts between equal protection and the police power which are not found in the Barbier case. In *Connolly* v. *Union Sewer Pipe Co.*,[8] the Court invalidated an Illinois antitrust statute because it exempted agricultural producers from its application. Although the specific ruling in this case has since been reversed,[9] the general principles underlying the decision have not been affected. Conflicts between equal protection and state power cannot be resolved merely by reference to the police power, because no constitutional right can be impaired or destroyed by the states, regardless of the source of power. Accordingly, legislation affecting health, morals, safety, and welfare is void if it denies equal protection of the laws. Legislation must be reasonable and not arbitrary

[7] *Ibid.*, 31, 32.   [8] 184 U.S. 540 (1902).
[9] *Tigner* v. *Texas,* 310 U.S. 141 (1940).

or capricious, and the question of reasonableness is one for judicial determination. Although classification of businesses for purposes of regulation is permissible, it, too, must meet the standard of reasonableness.

In 1910, in a decision otherwise unimportant, Justice Willis Van Devanter summarized the rules governing classification. First, the equal protection clause permits classification of property and callings for regulatory purposes when the classification is reasonable and not purely arbitrary. Second, classification, to be valid, does not have to be made "with mathematical nicety" or avoid in practice all inequality. Third, when classification is challenged, "if any state of facts reasonably can be conceived that would sustain it, the existence of that state of facts at the time the law was enacted must be assumed." Fourth, one who challenges the validity of classifications under the police power has the burden of proving them unreasonable and arbitrary.[10] As Justice Holmes once said, "The Fourteenth Amendment is not a pedagogical requirement of the impractical," and it is the constant business of the law to "draw distinctions of degree." [11]

In pursuance of these principles the Supreme Court has sustained scores of statutes or municipal ordinances classifying businesses or callings according to their nature, size, location, and relation to the public health, safety, and morals. The regulations cover a wide range of special disabilities, liabilities, exemptions, and immunities. Railroads and other public utilities and their real and imagined abuses as perceived by rustic legislators in the states have been the most frequent object of classification for purposes of state regulation. Although the Court has reinforced the requirements of due process of law by the ruling that the fixing of unjustly and unreasonably low rates by state agencies is a denial of

[10] *Lindsley* v. *Carbonic Natural Gas Co.*, 220 U.S. 61, 78–79 (1911).
[11] *Dominion Hotel Co.* v. *Arizona*, 249 U.S. 265, 268–69 (1919).

equal protection in that it compels one class to suffer a loss that others may gain,[12] it has sustained the great mass of special legislation directed against railroads, other utilities, and warehouses, so long as all within the same category are treated alike.[13] Thus, with few exceptions,[14] the Court has sustained statutes making railroad companies liable for attorneys' fees for plaintiffs in successful suits brought against them,[15] statutes requiring railroad companies and no others to cut Johnson grass and other noxious weeds along their rights of way and other lands,[16] and statutes subjecting railroads to burdens not imposed upon other common carriers.[17] Similarly the Court has recognized as reasonable, classifications of railroads and motor carriers on the basis of size, by sustaining exemptions of railroads of less than fifty miles in length from specific regulations [18] and exemptions of motor carriers hauling agricultural produce or farm machinery for

[12] *Reagan* v. *Farmers' Loan & Trust Co.,* 154 U.S. 362, 410 (1894).
[13] *Missouri Pacific R. Co.* v. *Humes,* 115 U.S. 512 (1885); *St. Louis & San Francisco Ry. Co.* v. *Matthews,* 165 U.S. 1 (1897); *St. Louis, I. M. & So. Ry. Co.* v. *Paul,* 173 U.S. 404 (1899).
[14] *Gulf, Colorado, & S. F. R. Co.* v. *Ellis,* 165 U.S. 150 (1897), in validating a provision for plaintiffs recovery of attorney's fees in addition to costs and damages. See also *Atchison, T. & S. F. R. Co.* v. *Vosburg,* 238 U.S. 56 (1915), and *Lake Shore & Michigan So. Ry. Co.* v. *Smith,* 173 U.S. 684 (1899), invalidating a Michigan statute requiring railroads to sell tickets for trips of 1,000 miles or more at less than regular rates for use by purchaser and his immediate family within a period of two years. The second decision was reversed in *Pennsylvania R. Co.* v. *Towers,* 245 U.S. 6 (1917).
[15] *Atchison, T. & S. F. R. Co.* v. *Matthews,* 174 U.S. 96 (1899); *Kansas City So. R. Co.* v. *Anderson,* 233 U.S. 325 (1914); *Missouri, K., & T. R. Co.* v. *Cade,* 233 U.S. 642 (1914); *Missouri K. & T. R. Co.* v. *Harris,* 234 U.S. 412 (1914); *Missouri Pacific R. Co.* v. *Larabee,* 234 U.S. 459 (1914); *Dohany* v. *Rogers,* 281 U.S. 362 (1930).
[16] *Missouri, K. & T. R. Co.* v. *May,* 194 U.S. 267 (1904). Here the Texas statute did not directly require railroads to cut the grass and Russian thistle, but made them liable to penalties to be paid owners of contiguous lands for permitting them to go to seed, provided the contiguous owner had kept his from going to seed. Justice Holmes, speaking for the Court, averred that for all the Court knew, railroads could be the most serious spreaders of the seeds of these noxious plants. See also *Chicago, Terre Haute, & S. R. Co.* v. *Anderson,* 242 U.S. 283 (1916).
[17] *Seaboard Air Line R. Co.* v. *Watson,* 287 U.S. 86 (1932).
[18] *New York, New Haven & H. R. Co.* v. *New York,* 165 U.S. 628 (1897); *Chi-*

local use from general regulations.[19] Banks, insurance companies, securities dealers, loan agencies, and warehouses have long been classified by state legislatures, not only in contrast to other forms of economic activity, but within specific categories. With few exceptions [20] all such classifications have been sustained by judicial recognition of differences between fire insurance and other types,[21] mutual and stock companies,[22] foreign and domestic companies,[23] and life and casualty insurance.[24]

With respect to trading in securities the Court has sustained far-reaching classifications drawing distinctions between types of securities, outright and margin sales, and the like, regardless of the lack of logic in the classification.[25] Similarly the Court has condoned legislative distinctions between large and small banks,[26] banks and loan companies,[27] and depositors and other creditors.[28]

Other than special regulation of pool rooms, saloons, milk distributors, physicians, osteopaths, and other callings or pro-

---

cago, R. I. & P. R. Co. v. *Arkansas*, 219 U.S. 453 (1911); *Chesapeake & Ohio R. Co.* v. *Conley*, 230 U.S. 513 (1913).

[19] *Sproles* v. *Binford*, 286 U.S. 374 (1932). See also *Stephenson* v. *Binford*, 287 U.S. 251 (1932); *Aero Mayflower Transit Co.* v. *Public Service Commission*, 295 U.S. 285 (1935); *Railway Express Agency* v. *New York*, 336 U.S. 106 (1949). All of these latter cases stress the special interest of the states and their subdivisions in the maintenance of highways or streets and the promotion of safety on them. The last decision sustained a New York city traffic regulation prohibiting vehicles used for hire from carrying advertising matter, but permitting it on delivery vehicles used by an owner in the usual course of business within specified limits.

[20] See, for example, *Hartford Steam Boiler I. & I. Co.* v. *Harrison*, 301 U.S. 459 (1937).

[21] *Orient Fire Ins. Co.* v. *Daggs*, 172 U.S. 557 (1899).

[22] *German Alliance Ins. Co.* v. *Lewis*, 233 U.S. 389 (1914).

[23] *Metropolitan Casualty Ins. Co.* v. *Brownell*, 294 U.S. 580 (1935).

[24] *Ibid.*

[25] *Hall* v. *Geiger-Jones Co.*, 242 U.S. 539 (1917). See also *Otis & Gassman* v. *Parker*, 187 U.S. 606 (1903).

[26] *Engel* v. *O'Malley*, 219 U.S. 128 (1911).

[27] *Griffith* v. *Connecticut*, 218 U.S. 263 (1910); *Mutual Loan Co.* v. *Martell*, 222 U.S. 225 (1911).

[28] *Assaria State Bank* v. *Dolley*, 219 U.S. 121 (1911). Here a Kansas statute gave preference to depositors over other creditors of banks.

fessions intimately bearing on the public health, safety, and morals,[29] many of the regulations challenged center on exemptions on the basis of size and location and distinctions between residents and nonresidents, foreign and domestic corporations, and corporations and natural persons. With a few exceptions [30] the Court has sustained the legislation in question. Exemptions from labor legislation of employers of less than a designated number of employees, of residents

[29] *Murphy* v. *California*, 225 U.S. 623 (1912), prohibiting the keeping of pool rooms for hire, but permitting them in hotels for registered guests; *Hayman* v. *Galveston*, 273 U.S. 414 (1927), exclusion of osteopaths from practice in a city hospital; *Collins* v. *Texas*, 223 U.S. 288 (1912), denial of license to osteopaths to practice medicine; *Crane* v. *Johnson*, 242 U.S. 349 (1917), exempting persons treating disease by prayer while requiring license of "trained" faith healers, on the basis of the difference between prayer and mental suggestion; *Eberle* v. *Michigan*, 232 U.S. 700 (1914), prohibiting sale of liquors by merchants generally, but permitting sale by druggists for "medicinal, mechanical, or scientific purposes"; *Borden's Farm Products Co.* v. *Ten Eyck*, 297 U.S. 251 (1936), sustaining price differential of milk up to one cent per quart in favor of dealers selling milk not having a well-advertised trade name, with the same differential in stores; but contrast with *Mayflower Farms* v. *Ten Eyck*, 297 U.S. 266 (1936), invalidating the denial of such differentials to persons entering the milk business after the enactment of the law. The Twenty-first Amendment has in effect deprived distillers, brewers, and vendors of alcoholic beverages of all protection against state action under the federal Constitution. See *Indianapolis Brewing Co.* v. *Liquor Control Commission*, 305 U.S. 391 (1939); *Mahoney* v. *Joseph Wines Corporation*, 304 U.S. 401 (1938). In their separate ways both milk and whiskey have been important ingredients in constitutional law.

[30] *Louis K. Liggett Co.* v. *Baldridge*, 278 U.S. 105 (1928), invalidating a Pennsylvania statute requiring drug stores, except those already established, to be owned by a licensed pharmacist, or, if owned by a corporation, all stockholders to be licensed pharmacists; *Frost* v. *Corporation Commission*, 278 U.S. 515 (1929), invalidating an Oklahoma statute distinguishing between cotton gins operated by corporations and those by co-operatives. These decisions have been shaken and narrowed by *Daniel* v. *Family Security Life Ins. Co.*, 336 U.S. 220 (1949), and *Asbury Hospital* v. *Cass County*, 326 U.S. 207 (1945). For an invalid distinction between foreign and domestic corporations, see *Kentucky Finance Corp.* v. *Paramount Auto Exchange Corp.*, 262 U.S. 544 (1923), but contrast with *Blake* v. *McClung*, 172 U.S. 239 (1898), and *Kane* v. *New Jersey*, 242 U.S. 160 (1916). For an important case invalidating a distinction on the basis of size, see *Cotting* v. *Godard*, 183 U.S. 79 (1901), in which the Court held unconstitutional a Kansas statute so drawn as to regulate a stockyards company in Kansas City while leaving stockyards in other cities or towns unregulated.

of cities on the basis of population, and the like, are fairly common.[31]

Two cases decided in 1955 and 1957 will suffice to illustrate the application of the equal protection clause to public regulation. In *Williamson* v. *Lee Optical Co.*[32] the Court unanimously sustained an Oklahoma statute prohibiting opticians from fitting or duplicating lenses in eye glasses without a prescription from an ophthalmologist or optometrist, while exempting sellers of ready-to-wear glasses from this requirement. According to Justice William O. Douglas, the equal protection clause prohibits only invidious discrimination, and that was not found to be present. Moreover, for all the record showed, the ready-to-wear branch of the business was unimportant.

Two years later, in *Morey* v. *Doud*,[33] invidious discrimination was found in an Illinois statute which required all firms issuing and selling money orders to obtain a license, while exempting the American Express Company from its provisions. In addition to the requirement of a license, all mail order companies except American Express were subjected to a comprehensive plan of regulation which included supplying information, maintaining a security fund ranging from

[31] *Walls* v. *Midland Carbon Co.*, 254 U.S. 300 (1920), sustaining regulation of gas wells within ten miles of incorporated town or plant; *Douglas* v. *New York, N. H. & H. R. Co.* 279 U.S. 377 (1929), sustaining distinction between foreign and domestic corporations. See also *Washington* ex rel. *Bond & Goodwin & Tucker* v. *Superior Court*, 289 U.S. 361 (1933); *Consolidated Coal Co.* v. *Illinois*, 185 U.S. 315 (1902); *McLean* v. *Arkansas*, 211 U.S. 539 (1909); *Jeffrey Mfg. Co.* v. *Blagg*, 235 U.S. 571 (1915), all sustaining exemptions of employers from labor regulations on the basis of a small designated number of employees; *Northwestern Laundry Co.* v. *Des Moines*, 239 U.S. 486 (1916), sustaining a statute prohibiting the emission of dense smoke in cities of more than 65,000 inhabitants; *Asbury Hospital* v. *Cass County*, 326 U.S. 207 (1945), sustaining a North Dakota statute requiring corporations to divest themselves of agricultural lands not necessary to the conduct of business. See also *Middleton* v. *Texas Power & Light Co.*, 249 U.S. 152 (1919), for a comprehensive scheme of valid exemptions in a workmen's compensation statute.

[32] 348 U.S. 483 (1955).   [33] 354 U.S. 457 (1957).

$3,000 to $25,000, carrying an insurance policy ranging from $2,500 to $35,000, conducting each exchange as a separate business unit independently of any other business, filing annual reports, and paying investigation fees. In addition to the rules stated above, the Court repeated the warning of earlier decisions [34] that discriminations of an unusual character are subject to careful scrutiny to determine whether they are obnoxious to the equal protection clause.

Six of the justices could find no reasonable basis in the distinction between American Express and other companies and regarded the discrimination as one placing American Express in a closed class with decided competitive advantages. Justices Hugo Black and Felix Frankfurter wrote separate dissents and Justice John M. Harlan joined the latter. Justice Frankfurter protested that law "reflects distinctions that exist in fact or at least appear to exist in the judgment of legislators" and that legislation as an essentially empirical enterprise addresses itself "to the more or less crude outside world and not to the neat logical models of the mind." Moreover, classification is inherent in legislation. "To recognize marked differences that exist in fact is living law; to disregard practical differences and concentrate on some abstract identities is lifeless logic." [35] The dissent and the majority opinions proceed from the same general rules, but they reach opposite results because neither the general contours of equal protection nor judicial glosses on it are subject to calculation in mathematical exactitude or logical symmetry. Hence the Court always has what Justice Holmes called "the sovereign prerogative of choice," with the result that in specific situations equal protection, like the rest of the Constitution, must take some chances.

The cases involving classification of property for purposes

---

[34] *Louisville Gas & Electric Co.* v. *Coleman*, 277 U.S. 32, 37, 38 (1928), and *Hartford S. B. I. & I. Co.* v. *Harrison*, 301 U.S. 459, 462 (1937).
[35] *Morey* v. *Doud*, 473.

of taxation corroborate Mr. Thurman Arnold's dictum that "taxation without litigation is tyranny," [36] but they add little to the principles enunciated by the Court in the cases dealing with regulation. Like the cases on regulation, and on similar principles, they accord to legislative bodies, assessors, and other tax officials a wide discretion to select, distinguish, and classify the objects of taxation so long as the classification is reasonable. With an awareness of the infirmities of legislators and tax assessors, the Court has consistently taken a practical view of taxation, so as to condone what Justice Joseph Mc-Kenna once called "rough accommodations—illogical . . . and unscientific," on the theory that what is best is not always discernible.[37] As Justice Holmes answered arguments against the assessment of land at full value without deducting the amount of the mortgage upon it, ". . . you cannot carry a constitution out with mathematical nicety to logical extremes. If you could we never should have heard of the police power. And this is still more true of taxation, which, in most communities, is a long way off from a logical and consistent theory." [38] The purpose of equal protection, according to Justice James C. McReynolds, is to secure every person against intentional and arbitrary discrimination, whether produced by the terms of the statute or by improper administration. Hence the intentional and systematic underassessment of the property of some is a denial of equal protection; [39] but mere errors of judgment will not support a claim of discrimination and, unless there is a showing of an intentional denial of equality, the good faith of tax officials and the validity of their action will be presumed.[40]

Accordingly, comparatively few important tax enactments and assessments have been invalidated as a denial of equal

[36] Thurman W. Arnold, *The Folklore of Capitalism* (New Haven, 1937), 324.
[37] *Metropolis Theater Co.* v. *Chicago*, 228 U.S. 61, 69–70 (1913).
[38] *Paddell* v. *City of New York*, 211 U.S. 446, 450 (1908).
[39] Citing *Raymond* v. *Chicago Union Transit Co.*, 207 U.S. 20, 35 (1907).
[40] *Sunday Lake Iron Co.* v. *Wakefield*, 247 U.S. 350, 353 (1918).

protection,[41] and many of these came in the fifteen years between 1922 and 1937, when a conservative Court was introducing a great variety of innovations to protect property and limit the powers of the states and Congress to govern and to tax—this without evoking protests from those pillars of society, who possess a monopoly of "conventional wisdom," [42] that the Court was invading states' rights or engaged in legislation. In general, although the Court has invalidated considerably more taxes or assessments than regulatory statutes as denials of equal protection, it has been somewhat indifferent to the cries of anguish from taxpayers, because it has not desired to become a national board of tax appeals and is not equipped to handle the multiplicity of special issues that arise out of the levying, assessment, and collection of taxes. Even so, the Court has emphasized that it will not condone in any area of governmental activity "clear and hostile dis-

---

[41] See, e.g., *Raymond v. Chicago Union Traction Co.,* 207 U.S. 20 (1907); *Southern R. Co. v. Greene,* 216 U.S. 400 (1910); *Gast Realty & Investment Co. v. Schneider Granite Co.,* 240 U.S. 55 (1916); *F. S. Royster Guano Co. v. Virginia,* 253 U.S. 412 (1920); *Bethlehem Motors Corp.* v. *Flynt,* 256 U.S. 421 (1921); *Sioux City Bridge Co. v. Dakota County,* 260 U.S. 441 (1923); *Thomas v. Kansas City Southern R. Co.,* 261 U.S. 481 (1923); *Hoeper v. Tax Commission,* 284 U.S. 206 (1931), Holmes, Brandeis, and Stone, dissenting; *Concordia Fire Insurance Co. v. Illinois,* 292 U.S. 535 (1934), Cardozo, Brandeis, and Stone, dissenting; *Valentine v. Great Atlantic & Pacific Tea Co.,* 299 U.S. 32 (1936), Cardozo and Brandeis dissenting; *Binney v. Long,* 299 U.S. 280 (1936), Cardozo and Brandeis, dissenting. Justice Stone did not participate in the last two cases. Taxes or assessments were also invalidated as denials of equal protection in *Kansas City Southern R. Co. v. Road Improvement District,* 256 U.S. 258 (1921); *Louisville Gas & Electric Co. v. Coleman,* 277 U.S. 32 (1928), over strong dissents by Holmes and Brandeis, who were joined by Stone; *Iowa–Des Moines National Bank v. Bennett,* 284 U.S. 239 (1931); *Stewart Dry Goods Co. v. Lewis,* 294 U.S. 550 (1935), with Cardozo, Brandeis, and Stone dissenting; *Colgate v. Harvey,* 296 U.S. 404 (1935), invoking the privileges and immunities clause of Article IV to reinforce equal protection, but reversed by *Madden v. Kentucky,* 309 U.S. 83 (1940); *Hanover Fire Ins. Co. v. Carr,* 272 U.S. 494 (1926); *Hopkins v. Southern California Telephone Co.,* 275 U.S. 393 (1927); *Cumberland Coal Co. v. Board of Revision,* 284 U.S. 23 (1931); *Air-Way Elec. Appliance Co. v. Day,* 266 U.S. 71 (1924); *Quaker City Cab Co. v. Pennsylvania,* 277 U.S. 389 (1928).

[42] The phrase is John Kenneth Galbraith's. See Chapter II, "The Concept of Conventional Wisdom," in his *The Affluent Society* (New York, 1958). Generally speaking, conventional wisdom is not wisdom at all.

criminations against particular persons and classes, especially such as are of an unusual character, unknown to the practice of our governments." [43]

Hence, classification for purposes of taxation must be reasonable; and arbitrary, oppressive, or capricious discriminations based on "differences of color, race, nativity, religious opinions, political affiliations, or other considerations having no possible connection with the duties of citizens as taxpayers . . . would be pure favoritism, and a denial of the equal protection of the laws to the less favored classes." [44] In other words, the vast range of the discretion of the legislature to classify property and callings does not include any power whatsoever to make distinctions between persons or classes on the basis of race, color, religion, or party membership, because such a basis is inherently unreasonable.

Despite a somewhat greater judicial vigilance over taxation in the 1920's and 1930's, when it invalidated a number of tax measures as denials of equal protection, the Court exhibited a high degree of judicial tolerance in sustaining state taxes of a discriminatory nature levied on chain stores during those years—except for a partial invalidation of the Florida tax because it was graduated not only according to the number of units in the chain, but increased the tax per unit if the chain operated in more than one county.[45] An Indiana chain store license tax, payable annually, which ranged from $25.00 per unit and was graduated according to the total units in the state, was sustained in *State Board of Tax Commissioners* v. *Jackson* [46] over the strenuous objections of Justices George Sutherland, Van Devanter, McReynolds, and Pierce Butler. The majority proceeded on the assumption that "the legislature is not confined merely to the value of the business taxed, but may have regard to other elements," including the

[43] *Bell's Gap R. Co.* v. *Pennsylvania,* 134 U.S. 232 (1890).
[44] *American Sugar Refining Co.* v. *Louisiana,* 179 U.S. 89, 92 (1900).
[45] *Louis K. Liggett Co.* v. *Lee,* 288 U.S. 517 (1933).
[46] 283 U.S. 527, 536 (1931).

methods of buying and selling employed by chain stores and their comparative advantages.

Judicial tolerance of chain store taxation reached its peak in *Great Atlantic & Pacific Tea Co.* v. *Grosjean*,[47] at the beginning of the constitutional revolution of 1937. Here the Court sustained the Louisiana chain store tax which was graduated, not according to the number of units in the state, but according to the total within the United States, at rates which ranged from $10.00 per unit annually for the small local chains to $550.00 per unit for chains of more than five hundred units, so that the tax, in addition to discriminating against chains generally, imposed a double inequality on large national chains. With Justice Van Devanter not participating, the other three irreconcilables, who refused to accept some governmental developments in the twentieth century, dissented with futility. Since 1937 the Court has shown a decided indifference to the complaints of taxpayers, so that there has been a steady diminution of cases assailing taxes as denials of equal protection, and it is a rarity for a tax to be invalidated as a denial of equal protection.[48]

To emphasize the obvious, the cases involving equal protection and economic interests display great deference to the judgment of legislatures. Almost always, in contrast to most of the cases dealing with racial discrimination, the Court has followed the rational basis test by presuming the reasonableness of the classification in the absence of a clear showing of invidious discrimination. A statute need not be logical, it need not even be just. Practicality is the theme of the Court. In the words of Justice Holmes, the Fourteenth Amendment is not a requirement of the impracticable. And "the equal protection of the laws does not mean that all occupations that are called by the same name must be treated in the same

[47] 301 U.S. 412 (1937). See also *Fox* v. *Standard Oil Co.*, 294 U.S. 87 (1935), which sustained a West Virginia chain store tax.
[48] Two such rarities are *Wheeling Steel Corp.* v. *Glander*, 337 U.S. 562 (1949), and *Hillsborough Township* v. *Cromwell*, 326 U.S. 620 (1946).

way." [49] Even a consistent antagonist of governmental action like Justice David Brewer could observe that "the very idea of classification is that of inequality," [50] and recognize that "mere inequalities or exemptions in the matter of state taxation are not forbidden by the Federal Constitution." [51]

If the Court has occasionally been indifferent to the wails of the taxpayer seeking a refuge within the ample folds of equal protection, the judges have shown an almost josephic aversion to women. Although numerous discriminations in favor of or against women have existed in the common law and statutes of the states since the ratification of the Fourteenth Amendment, very few have been challenged as denials of equal protection, and none has been invalidated on this ground. Whether this means that women have been happy with such discriminations, or that they have taken literally St. Paul's admonition to submit themselves unto their husbands as unto the Lord, presents a question full of speculative interest and possibilities, but it is hardly relevant to the judicial development of equal protection. It is worthy of passing notice, however, that the first challenge of a personal and class discrimination made in the Supreme Court was made in behalf of the equality of women before the law in *Bradwell* v. *Illinois*.[52]

The case involved the validity of a rule of the Supreme Court of Illinois which excluded women from the practice of law before its bar. Matt H. Carpenter, who had argued for a restrictive interpretation of the amendment in the Slaughterhouse Cases during the same term of court, was obsequious to his own and his clients' interests in contending

[49] *Dominion Hotel Co.* v. *Arizona*, 249 U.S. 265, 269 (1919).
[50] *Atchison, T. & S. F. R. Co.* v. *Matthews*, 174 U.S. 96, 106 (1899), quoted with approval by Justice McKenna in *International Harvester Co.* v. *Missouri*, 234 U.S. 199 (1914).
[51] *Beers* v. *Glynn*, 211 U.S. 477, 485 (1909). See also *Rosenthal* v. *New York*, 226 U.S. 260, 271 (1912); *Chicago Dock & Canal Co.* v. *Fraley*, 228 U.S. 680, 687 (1913); *Crescent Cotton Oil Co.* v. *Mississippi*, 257 U.S. 129 (1921).
[52] 16 Wall. 130 (1873).

for a broader scope in this case. Although he based his argument largely on the privileges and immunities clause, which he had helped to emasculate in the Slaughterhouse Cases, he quoted Justice Field [53] to the effect that all callings and honors are alike open to everyone and that in the protection of this right all are equal before the law. Then he asserted that a legislature or a court cannot impose qualifications for the practice of law which can never be met or which exclude a whole class. This part of his argument was based on his assumption that the equal protection clause "protects every citizen, black or white, male or female." [54] The Court, speaking through Justice Miller, disposed of the case by ruling against female lawyers on the rationale of the Slaughterhouse Cases; and Justice Joseph Bradley, one of the dissenters in those cases, wrote a separate concurrence, in which Justices Field and Noah Swayne joined, to dispose of the issue on the basis of women's status in the common law. Otherwise, the equal protection argument went unanswered.

Two years later, in *Minor* v. *Happersett*,[55] the Court unanimously sustained a Missouri statute excluding women from the suffrage. Chief Justice Waite asserted with confidence that women are persons and even citizens of the United States. Nevertheless, they had no right to vote by virtue of any privilege or immunity of citizenship. Although the opinion did not involve the equal protection clause, Chief Justice Waite, in discussing citizenship, emphasized the reciprocal nature of allegiance and protection and thereby affirmed one of the contentions of the Radical Republicans of the Thirty-ninth and succeeding Congresses. The citizen owes the nation allegiance, the nation owes the citizen protection. "Allegiance and protection are, in this connection, reciprocal obligations. The one is a compensation for the other; allegiance for protection and protection for allegiance."

[53] *Cummings* v. *Missouri,* 4 Wall. 277, 321, 322 (1867).
[54] *Bradwell* v. *Illinois,* 16 Wall. 130.   [55] 21 Wall. 162, 165–66 (1875).

In two other ways the Minor and Bradwell cases are in accord with the expectation of the framers. The Minor case confirms their argument that the first section of the Fourteenth Amendment is not concerned with political rights such as the suffrage, and the Bradwell case sanctions the denials of the Radicals, in replies to their opponents, that the amendment would repeal all state laws containing discriminations because of sex.

State legislation limiting the hours of work of women and providing for conditions of labor, in specified employments not applicable to men has encountered no constitutional obstacles with respect to equal protection. Such legislation is a common part of American labor law and has been sustained on the assumption that what all men know, judges must be presumed to know. Hence the Court has taken judicial notice of the physical differences between men and women, the physical frailty of women, their childbearing function, and the especial hazards which beset them, particularly the working girl, for whom the legendary protection of heaven is deemed insufficient.[56]

An extreme form of discrimination against women in employment is illustrated by Goesaert v. Cleary.[57] As a part of its system for controlling the sale of intoxicating liquors, the Michigan legislature provided for the licensing of all bartenders in cities with a population of fifty thousand or more, but forbade the licensing of any female bartender except the wife or daughter of the male owner of a licensed saloon or bar. Fully equal to the occasion, Justice Frankfurter pointed to "the ale wife, sprightly and ribald, in Shakespeare," and prominent in the social life of England centuries before him, and argued that the Fourteenth Amend-

[56] Muller v. Oregon, 208 U.S. 412 (1908); Miller v. Wilson, 236 U.S. 373 (1915); Bosley v. McLaughlin, 236 U.S. 385 (1915); Radice v. New York, 264 U.S. 292 (1924). Some of these cases also involve classifications of employments and businesses in addition to those based on sex.
[57] 335 U.S. 464 (1948).

ment did not tear up history by the roots. "The fact that women now have achieved virtues that men have long claimed as their prerogatives and now indulge in vices that men have long practiced, does not preclude the States from drawing a sharp line between the sexes, certainly in such matters as the regulation of the liquor traffic." He then referred to the legislative belief that the oversight assured through ownership of a bar by the barmaid's husband or father "minimizes hazards that may confront a barmaid without such protecting oversight." [58] In dissent, Justices Douglas, Wiley Rutledge, and Frank Murphy were unimpressed by the perils besetting husbandless and fatherless barmaids, but they completely overlooked the tendency of the statute to create an almost closed employment for men, and protested that the statute discriminated against female bar owners by forbidding them to work themselves or to employ their daughters as barmaids.

These decisions, buttressed by the common law, long established legislative principles, and social history, suggest an almost unlimited range of legislative discretion in making distinctions on the basis of sex in all phases of governmental activity. Sex is the only quality inseparable from the person that affords such possibilities, although age, imbecility, and insanity play their role in determining rights under the vestiges of the old concept of status. The principles enunciated in these cases and in the law generally are certainly broad enough to sustain segregation of the sexes in public education, subject to the provision of adequate curricula and physical facilities, the total disqualification of women in some employments and professions, and perhaps even a return by the states to the Blackstonian conception that when a man and woman marry, they become one, and that one is the husband.

Interesting and important as some of the miscellaneous

[58] *Ibid.*, 465, 466.

cases are, they add little to the judicial application of the
equal protection clause, and they may be ignored save for a
few which reflect the Court's concern for basic personal rights
and its comparative indifference to political rights. In *Skinner*
v. *Oklahoma* [59] the Court invalidated an Oklahoma statute
providing for the compulsory sterilization of habitual criminals because it excluded the genteel offense of embezzlement from its definition of crimes "amounting to felonies
involving moral turpitude." Justice Douglas and five other
judges believed embezzlement to be as serious as stealing
chickens and held the exemption of embezzlers an invidious
discrimination against other common criminals, thereby
leaving the impression that a sterilization law operating
equally on all felons would be valid. Such an implication was
too much for Chief Justice Harlan F. Stone, who thought the
law totally bad on due process grounds, and for Justice
Robert H. Jackson, who found it bad under both due process
and equal protection. The opinions of all three are characterized by a solicitude for the basic human right of self-
perpetuation of the race at a time when the Nazis were
conducting their experiments in genocide.

On the other hand, the Court, in two fairly recent cases,
has shown a bland unconcern for equitable representation
in state legislatures and Congress and for the principle that
every man's or woman's vote shall count for one, no more
and no less. Thus in *Colegrove* v. *Green*,[60] the Court, by a
six-to-three vote, held that inequalities in the apportionment
of congressional representation in Illinois which greatly
favored residents of rural areas and small towns over those
of urban areas presented a political question which the Court
could not decide. Similarly, in *South* v. *Peters*,[61] the Court
ruled that Georgia's version of the rotten borough—its county
unit vote system for nominating candidates for public office,
whereby the vote of a clay-eater on some tobacco road in the

[59] 316 U.S. 535 (1942).   [60] 328 U.S. 549 (1946).   [61] 339 U.S. 276 (1950).

least populous of counties was equal in 1950 to 120 votes in populous, sophisticated Atlanta—posed a political question beyond judicial scrutiny. As Justices Douglas and Black pointed out, the scheme not only perpetrated a gross discrimination on urban voters, but also on the heavy Negro population in the cities.

In *Snowden* v. *Hughes* [62] the Court asserted that although political rights are protected against unreasonable discrimination, they are entitled to no more or no less protection than other rights, with the result that the refusal of a canvassing board to certify as the nominee a person who had won the nomination was held no denial of equal protection. This holding was based on the ground that the unlawful administration of a valid statute is no denial of equal protection in the absence of a clear showing of discrimination.

Most of the cases involving equal protection and legislative power to formulate rules of evidence and legal procedure and modes of punishment are relatively unimportant, and accord to legislatures a broad discretion to vary rules of procedure and evidence within specified areas of the state, such as cities,[63] and with respect to the nature of the offense or legal action.[64] But there have been some important developments in this area since 1942. The rulings in *Cochran* v. *Kansas* [65] and *Dowd* v. *United States* ex rel. *Cook* [66] that the equal protection of the laws is denied a prisoner when he is not permitted, by prison rules or otherwise, to take an appeal

---

[62] 321 U.S. 1 (1944). See also *McDougall* v. *Green*, 335 U.S. 281 (1948).

[63] *Missouri (Bowman)* v. *Lewis*, 101 U.S. 22 (1880); *Salsburg* v. *Maryland*, 346 U.S. 545 (1954); *Minnesota* ex rel. *Pearson* v. *Superior Court*, 309 U.S. 270 (1940). See also *Ohio* ex rel. *Bryant* v. *Akron Metropolitan Park Dist.*, 281 U.S. 74 (1930). *Milwaukee Electric Ry. & L. Co.* v. *Wisconsin*, 252 U.S. 100 (1920), is interesting for the holding that equal protection is not denied by irreconcilable judicial decisions, which the Court affirmed need not be uniform. See also the Bryant case, cited immediately before this case.

[64] *Collins* v. *Johnston*, 237 U.S. 503 (1915); *Graham* v. *West Virginia*, 224 U.S. 616 (1912); *Finley* v. *California*, 222 U.S. 28 (1911); *Howard* v. *Fleming*, 191 U.S. 126 (1903); *Mallett* v. *North Carolina*, 181 U.S. 589 (1901); *Pennsylvania* ex rel. *Sullivan* v. *Ashe*, 302 U.S. 51 (1937).

[65] 316 U.S. 255 (1942).   [66] 340 U.S. 206 (1951).

until it is too late, while persons not in prison can appeal, are not only a reaffirmation of the equality of all men before the law, but are also an emphasis on the right of a person to protection in court as an echo of the idealism of Magna Carta and the provisions of some state constitutions. When placed alongside such cases as *Barbier* v. *Connolly,*[67] *Ex parte Young,*[68] and *Truax* v. *Corrigan,*[69] which in their own ways emphasize the right of recourse to courts for the vindication of rights and the prevention or redress of wrongs, these decisions could help to restore the word *protection* to the Fourteenth Amendment.

Even more important to the attainment of equality before the law is *Griffin* v. *Illinois,*[70] in which the Court attempted to mitigate the inequalities inherent in poverty with respect to taking criminal appeals. The case involved an Illinois statute which provides that indigent defendants may procure a free transcript of the trial record, in capital cases only, in order to obtain a review of constitutional issues, but not of other alleged trial errors. Justice Black and Justice Frankfurter, in a separate concurrence, ruled the denial of a free transcript to the defendants, who had been convicted of armed robbery, a violation of due process and equal protection. Chief Justice Earl Warren and Justices Douglas and Tom C. Clark concurred in Justice Black's opinion. In addition to these clauses Justice Black invoked Magna Carta to condemn invidious distinctions between persons and groups of persons and to affirm "that all people charged with

[67] 113 U.S. 27 (1885).

[68] 209 U.S. 123, 145–47 (1908). Here the Court held unconstitutional a Minnesota rate statute, because the penalties imposed for violation of its provisions were regarded as too excessive to permit violation and then recourse to the courts. The Court averred that equal protection means recourse to the courts.

[69] 257 U.S. 312 (1921). Here the Court invalidated an Arizona statute limiting the power of state courts to issue injunctions in labor disputes, on the ground that due process and equal protection require a minimum of protection—in this instance, recourse to the courts for an injunction.

[70] 351 U.S. 12 (1956).

crime must, so far as the law is concerned, 'stand on an equality before the bar of justice in every American court.' " [71] Justice Black went on to conclude that there is "no equal justice where the kind of trial a man gets depends on the amount of money he has." [72] The principles of Justice Black's opinion in *Griffin* v. *Illinois* were reiterated and reaffirmed by a clear majority of the Court in *Burns* v. *Ohio*.[73] How much farther the Court can go in the elimination of economic inequalities in the administration of justice raises many complicated questions for which constitutional law and political science have no facile answer. The fact is that by 1959 a clear majority of the Court was committed to the elimination of some economic inequalities from the administration of the criminal law.

Except for the importance of these cases, most of the others classified as "miscellaneous" are no more important than those dealing with secret societies. Even so, those who are interested in the mystical brotherhood of Greek-letter fraternities or the black magic of the Ku Klux Klan must regard it as melancholy that the equal protection clause affords no aid or comfort to such organizations. In 1915 the Court sustained a Mississippi statute prohibiting Greek-letter fraternities in state institutions of higher education and requiring applicants for admission to state colleges to renounce allegiance to and affiliation with a fraternity, while permitting brothers already enrolled to continue their membership so long as they conducted themselves "with that decorum always expected of Southern gentlemen." [74] Similarly, in 1928 the Court sustained the application to the Ku Klux Klan of a New York statute which required secret organizations to register and file reports with the secretary of state, but which exempted labor organizations and benevolent societies like

[71] *Ibid.*, 17, quoting *Chambers* v. *Florida,* 309 U.S. 227, 241 (1940).
[72] *Griffin* v. *Illinois,* 351 U.S. 12, 19.   [73] 360 U.S. 252 (1959).
[74] *Waugh* v. *Trustees of the University of Mississippi,* 237 U.S. 589 (1915).

the Masons and Odd Fellows, Eagles, Elk, and other fauna
which are impressive testimony of the American genius in
forming and joining associations.[75] Other miscellaneous cases
are equally trivial; and however true the maxim, *"De minimis
non curat lex,"* may be of the law generally, it is not always
true of constitutional law, which certainly deals with trifles
in a significant number of cases involving the great concept
of equal protection of the laws.

[75] *New York* ex rel. *Bryant* v. *Zimmerman,* 278 U.S. 63 (1928).

CHAPTER FOUR

Judicial Contraction of the Equal Protection Clause, 1873-1935

AFTER THESE JUDICIAL DIGRESSIONS
we now come to the central core of the equal protection
clause, that is, its application to discriminations based on
race or color and the power of Congress and the federal
courts to condemn them. Out of a tender regard for federalism as it existed before the Civil War, Justice Miller and a
majority of the Court rendered the privileges and immunities
clause of the Fourteenth Amendment almost meaningless
in the Slaughterhouse Cases [1] by holding that it was never

[1] 16 Wall. 36 (1873). Justice Miller's restrictive interpretation of the Fourteenth
Amendment has frequently been criticized. One of the more pungent criti-
cisms is that of John W. Burgess, *Political Science and Comparative Constitutional Law* (2 vols., Boston, 1890), I, 225–26. The magisterial Burgess in-
toned:
"I say that if history has taught anything in political science, it is that
civil liberty is national in its origin, content and sanction. I now go further,
and I affirm that if there is but a single lesson to be learned from the history
of the United States, it is this. Seventy years of debate and four years of
terrible war turn substantially upon this issue, in some part or other; and
when the Nation triumphed in the great appeal to arms, and addressed itself
to the work of readjusting the forms of law to the now undoubted conditions
of fact, it gave its first attention to the nationalization in constitutional law
of the domain of civil liberty. There is no doubt that those who framed the
thirteenth and fourteenth amendments intended to occupy the whole

82

the purpose of the amendment to federalize the privileges and immunities of state citizenship and transfer their custody to the federal courts.

The language of his opinion, therefore, is totally different from that of the framers of the Fourteenth Amendment in the Thirty-ninth Congress. For judicial expressions similar to those of the framers in these cases, we have to turn to the dissenting opinions and, in particular, to that of Justice Field, a states'-rights Democrat who, nevertheless, occasionally gave civil rights a priority over what Justice Holmes once called "the invisible radiation from the general terms of the 10th Amendment." [2] Justice Field reviewed to some extent the debate on the Civil Rights Act of 1866 and the Fourteenth Amendment and invoked the Declaration of Independence and *Corfield* v. *Coryell*,[3] in exact parallel to the arguments of the Radical Republicans, to contend that "full and equal benefit of all laws and proceedings for the security of person and property" is a privilege or immunity of citizenship, and that the privileges and immunities clause of Section 1 protected the equal rights of all citizens of the United States against hostile or discriminatory state legislation.[4]

Justice Bradley emphasized the Declaration of Independence even more and, like Justice Field, linked equality before the law with the privileges and immunities of United

ground and thought they had done so. The opposition charged that these amendments would nationalize the whole sphere of civil liberty; the majority accepted the view; and the legislation of Congress for their elaboration and enforcement proceeded upon that view. In the face of all these well known facts it was hardly to be doubted that . . . this great body [the Supreme Court] would unanimously declare the whole domain of civil liberty to be under its protection against both the general government and the commonwealths. Great, therefore, was the surprise when . . . the decision in the Slaughterhouse Cases was announced. . . ." After further discussion of the decision Burgess pronounced it "entirely erroneous" from whatever view he regarded it, "from the historical, political, or juristic" (I, 228). Footnotes omitted.

[2] *Missouri* v. *Holland*, 252 U.S. 416, 434 (1920).
[3] 6 Fed. Cas. No. 3230 (1823). [4] Slaughterhouse Cases, 98–110.

States citizens. He was not impressed with Justice Miller's fears that a broad interpretation of the amendment would impair or destroy the federal system. Without delineating the scope of congressional power, he thought as a practical matter that little legislation would be necessary to implement its provisions, and he regarded any increase in the amount of business of the federal courts as possibly negligible or at least inconsequential.[5] Neither of these judges discussed the equal protection clause, apparently because of their belief that equality before the law was a right of citizenship, and the challenged statute did not affect protection. Justice Swayne did mention equal protection in his dissent and, like Bingham in Congress, argued that the purpose of the amendment was to supply a want of federal power to provide protection against wrong and oppression by the states.[6]

The restrictive interpretation of privileges and immunities in the Slaughterhouse Cases did not touch equal protection or the power of Congress to provide it, but it heralded restrictions that were soon to come. In 1873 more than one hundred residents of Louisiana were indicted for violating the Enforcement Act of 1870, which imposed heavy penalties on persons going in disguise on public highways or conspiring to injure or threaten any citizen with intent to impair his rights under the Constitution and laws of the United States. Of the eight who went to trial on charges of conspiracy to injure, oppress, and intimidate two Negroes, three were convicted, but their convictions were reversed in *United States* v. *Cruikshank*,[7] because of faulty indictments. Chief Justice Waite, speaking for seven other judges, went far beyond the necessities of the case to give a very narrow construction of the due process and equal protection clauses. Expounding theories of dual federalism, which differed in no way from those of Chief Justice Taney, the Court ignored the changes wrought by civil war and the ensuing amend-

[5] *Ibid.*, 115–24.   [6] *Ibid.*, 129.   [7] 92 U.S. 542 (1876).

ments to the Constitution by declaring that the Fourteenth Amendment added nothing to "the rights of one citizen as against another" and simply furnished "an additional guaranty against any encroachment by the States upon the fundamental rights which belong to every citizen as a member of society." Although the Court admitted that every republican government is in duty bound to protect every citizen in the enjoyment of equality of rights, that duty was originally assumed by the states and remained there. "The only obligation resting upon the United States is to see that the States do not deny the right. This the Amendment guaranties, but no more. The power of the National Government is limited to the enforcement of this guaranty." [8]

On the basis of the restrictive decision of the Slaughterhouse Cases, it is not surprising that the Court reached this conclusion. What is surprising is the concurring opinion of Justice Nathan Clifford, a states'-rights Democrat, which would have confined the decision solely to defects in the indictment, to the exclusion of constitutional issues, and the silent acquiescence of Justices Field, Swayne, and Bradley in the majority opinion. Indeed, the concern which these judges expressed for a broad interpretation in the Slaughterhouse Cases and their tacit indifference to it here can only be explained by the cynical surmise that these judges were more interested in rights of property than in rights of persons, a surmise which has some evidence to support it.

Even so, Chief Justice Waite's discourse on the scope of federal power could be dismissed as obiter dictum or as a tortuous exercise in constitutional exegesis if this case stood alone. But it does not stand alone. The dicta of the Court

---

[8] *Ibid.*, 554–55. The Chief Justice emphasized the dualism of citizenship and rights enunciated in the Slaughterhouse Cases and dualism of government in the American federal system. Although he repeated the old principle with respect to the mutuality of allegiance and protection, he concluded that the duty of a government to afford protection is limited by the power it possesses for that purpose. (549).

in the Cruikshank case, restrictive of federal power, as it sometimes happens with dicta, became a rule of law seven years later in *United States* v. *Harris*,[9] in which the Court invalidated Section 2 of the Ku Klux Klan Act of 1871, which was almost identical to the provision of the Enforcement Act of 1870 at issue in the Cruikshank case. In the Harris case the indictment of twenty persons for killing a Negro and beating others while they were in custody of a West Tennessee sheriff was carefully drawn, and there was no way of avoiding the constitutional issue.

As spokesman for the Court, Justice William B. Woods declared that the purpose of the first section of the amendment was to restrict state action and that of the fifth to vest power in Congress to correct state laws not in conformity with the first section. In other words, the amendment condemned only positive actions of the states and not acts of omission, and the power of Congress was confined to the enactment of legislation corrective only of positive hostile and discriminatory state action. Justice Woods quoted from the circuit court opinion of Justice Bradley in the Cruikshank case to the effect that the amendment "is a guaranty of protection against the acts of the State Government itself . . . against the exertion of arbitrary and tyrannical power on the part of the Government and Legislature of the State" and "not a guaranty against the commission of individual offenses." [10]

Hence, according to Justice Bradley, the power of Congress to enforce the amendment did not authorize it to perform a duty which the amendment required the states to perform. Other cases were cited by Justice Woods to confine the amendment to condemning state action exclusively. Because no unequal state law was involved and because the state had recognized and endeavored to protect the rights of the persons

[9] 106 U.S. 629 (1883).
[10] *Ibid.*, 638, quoting *United States* v. *Cruikshank,* 1 Woods 316 (1874).

concerned, there was no denial of equal protection and no power on the part of Congress to supplement what proved to be inadequate state protection. This conclusion was based upon the following construction of the amendment: ". . . when the State has been guilty of no violation of its provisions; when it has not made or enforced any law abridging the privileges or immunities of citizens of the United States; when no one of its departments has deprived any person of life, liberty or property, without due process of law, nor denied to any person within its jurisdiction the equal protection of the laws; when, on the contrary, the laws of the State, as enacted by its legislative and construed by its judicial and administered by its executive departments, recognize and protect the rights of all persons, the Amendment imposes no duty and confers no power upon Congress." [11] Justice John M. Harlan, a newcomer to the Court in 1877, dissented without an opinion.

The contraction of the scope of the Fourteenth Amendment and the powers thereunder through the gradual process of judicial attrition continued in the Civil Rights Cases,[12] in which the Supreme Court held unconstitutional the first section of the Civil Rights Act of 1875, which prohibited discrimination against persons because of race or color by inns, public conveyances, theaters, and other places of public amusement. Justice Bradley, who was one of the architects of a narrow construction of the amendment with respect to racial discrimination and of a broad one as regards property rights, spoke for the Court and emphasized that it was only state or official action of a particular kind which the amendment prohibited, and not individual invasion of private rights; that is, he construed the equal protection clause to mean equality before the law in the sense that no state can make or enforce unequal laws. The whole power of Congress

[11] *United States* v. *Harris,* 106 U.S. 629, 639.
[12] 109 U.S. 3 (1883).

under the fifth section was confined to the enactment of legislation corrective of unequal state laws or discriminatory action by state officials. Otherwise, he reasoned, Congress would have the power to enact a code of municipal law for the protection of all private rights. Congress, therefore, had no secondary power to protect equality in the enjoyment of rights, even in the event of failure of the states to provide protection, and could intervene only when some state law had been passed or some state action taken that was adverse to the rights guaranteed by the amendment.

In turn, discrimination practiced by inns, public conveyances, and theaters was regarded as purely private in character despite the special status of public carriers and inns under the common law and the franchises and special privileges granted the former. The validity of federal prohibition of such discrimination would have to assume the power of Congress to legislate generally on private discrimination, and Justice Bradley found such an assumption "unsound" and "repugnant to the 10th Amendment." Hence, the wrongful acts of individual persons "unsupported by state authority in the shape of laws, customs or judicial or executive proceedings" could not impair rights guaranteed by the Constitution. Wrongs committed against persons without the sanction of the state would be protected by state law exclusively and their redress found by recourse to state law. The legislation in question was regarded as primary and direct and as superseding state legislation on the same subject. Nor was the legislation valid under the Thirteenth Amendment as the removal of an involuntary servitude.

The key to Justice Bradley's reasoning is perhaps to be found in the third paragraph from the end of his opinion, where he observed: "When a man has emerged from slavery, and by the aid of beneficent legislation has shaken off the inseparable concomitants of that state, there must be some stage in the progress of his elevation when he takes the rank of a mere citizen, and ceases to be the special favorite of the laws, and when his rights, as a citizen or a man, are to be protected in the ordinary modes by which other men's rights are protected." [13] The Negro a "special favorite of the laws"! Incredible as it is, not only the Court but a considerable portion of the public believed in it, as reflected by the Democratic congressional victories in 1874 and later years, by expressions of weariness with the solicitude for Negro rights expressed in editorials and campaign oratory, and, finally, by the desire of men in the Gilded Age to reap the material harvest of the philosophy of acquisition and enjoyment, unhampered by concern for social evils and private wrongs.

In a lengthy dissent, not entirely free of infirmities, Justice Harlan pierced the logic of the majority opinion. With righteous malice he cited *Prigg* v. *Pennsylvania* [14] and found it ironic that in the absence of an express delegation of power to Congress to provide for the return of fugitive slaves, it could enact comprehensive legislation to that end, while with express power to enforce constitutional rights under the Thirteenth and Fourteenth Amendments, it lacked the power to preserve freedom. He argued that racial discrimination by businesses of a public character or by a public corporation was both an unconstitutional servitude under the Thirteenth Amendment and a denial of that equality of right which was a privilege of citizenship under the Fourteenth. Although he did not accept the majority's limitation of the application of the amendment to state action or proceedings, he did argue that action by inns, carriers, and theaters is state action. A railroad is a public highway even when privately owned; and because it is a function of government to maintain highways, a private corporation which maintains them is an agent of the state performing state functions.

He found this line of reasoning applicable to inns and

[13] *Ibid.*, 25.   [14] 16 Pet. 539 (1842).

cited the duty of innkeepers under the common law to accommodate all travelers when they had sufficient room. With respect to places of public amusement Justice Harlan contended that those established and maintained under public licenses enjoyed a special status which required them to treat equally all members of the public which granted the license, and he also invoked the concept of business clothed with a public interest. Exemption from racial discrimination is a privilege of citizenship which in itself connotes equality of civil rights of every race in every state. "It is fundamental in American citizenship that, in respect of such rights, there shall be no discrimination by the State or its officers, or by individuals or corporations exercising public functions or authority, against any citizen because of his race or previous condition of servitude."

Justice Harlan found the confinement of congressional power to legislation corrective of state action unauthorized by the text of the first and fifth sections of the amendment. Corrective legislation might be sufficient in some circumstances; in others, "primary direct legislation," as he called it, would be required. In any event the amendment made Congress and not the courts the judge of what legislation may be appropriate.[15] Under the majority opinion he contended that congressional power had been limited rather than enlarged by the amendment and that the policy of the federal government since its organization had been reversed. Justice Harlan distinguished between social and legal rights and argued that the Act of 1875 was designed to protect legal rights. Among these he included the right of Negroes to use public highways in the same way as white citizens, to use public streets, turnpikes, public markets, and post offices, "to sit in a public building with others, of whatever race." Finally, Justice Harlan could not perceive the Negro as "the special favorite of the laws." What he saw was an intolerable

[15] Civil Rights Cases, 109 U.S. 3, 48, 51.

class tyranny, "ubiquitous in its operation," and weighing most heavily perhaps on those whose " 'obscurity or distance would withdraw themselves from the notice of a single despot.' " Today, he said, it is the colored race which is denied fundamental rights by public corporations; in the future some other race may "fall under the ban of race discrimination." If the Civil War amendments are to be enforced according to the intent of their framers, "there cannot be in this Republic, any class of human beings in practical subjection to another class, with power in the latter to dole out to the former just such privileges as they may choose to grant." [16]

The decision of the Supreme Court in the Civil Rights Cases has been subjected to serious criticism at various times, but it has never been reversed. It has been shaken seriously in a number of cases applying the general antidiscrimination clause of the Interstate Commerce Act so as to protect Negroes on interstate railways against discrimination in dining and sleeping cars, and in the cases taking a much broader view of state action since the 1940's. If it is true that the purpose of the Fourteenth Amendment was to empower Congress, among other things, to exercise a secondary authority to protect fundamental constitutional rights and to enforce equality of right in the event of failure of the states to exercise their primary responsibility to do so, then the decision in the Civil Rights Cases was an unnecessary departure from the Constitution. Moreover, neither Justice Bradley nor Justice Harlan gave any evidence of having read the legislative history of the amendment or the Act of 1875, and the same can be said of arguments of counsel on the basis of their sterile summary in the reports. However restrictive of the scope of the amendment the decision was, it condemned in unqualified and emphatic terms all discriminations of race or color by state laws or by state officials

[16] *Ibid.*, 62.

acting under the color of authority, even in violation of state law, so as to reaffirm at least the absolute equality of all persons before the law.

In so doing the Court was following a number of decisions rendered three years earlier, in 1880, which was a significant year in the judicial development of the equal protection clause. In *Strauder* v. *West Virginia* [17] the Supreme Court, over the silent dissents of Justices Clifford and Field, declared unconstitutional a state statute disqualifying Negroes from service on juries and grand juries as a denial of the equal protection of the laws. More important than the ruling was Justice William Strong's reasoning, which, although it was somewhat lacking in its discussion of the history of the amendment, unequivocally condemned all state-imposed discriminations because of race and left intact a greater degree of congressional discretion in the enforcement of equality than that permitted subsequently in the Civil Rights Cases, without, of course, resolving that issue. In the words of Justice Strong, the amendment was "designed to assure to the colored race the enjoyment of all the civil rights that under the law are enjoyed by white persons, and to give to that race the protection of the General Government, in that enjoyment, whenever it should be denied by the States."

He went on to declare by questions that equal protection means that the law shall be the same for the black as for the white, that "all persons, whether colored or white, shall stand equal before the laws of the States." Then he continued in language reminiscent of the framers: "The words of the Amendment, it is true, are prohibitory, but they contain a necessary implication of a positive immunity, or right, most valuable to the colored race—the right to exemption from unfriendly legislation against them distinctively as colored; exemption from legal discriminations, implying inferiority

[17] 100 U.S. 303 (1880).

in civil society, lessening the security of their enjoyment of the rights which others enjoy, and discriminations which are steps towards reducing them to the condition of a subject race." [18] How different is this sentiment from that of three years later, when it is proclaimed that the time must come when the Negro shall cease to be "the special favorite of the laws," and Congress is confined exclusively to the enactment of remedial legislation against unequal state action!

On the same day the Court also decided *Virginia* v. *Rives* [19] and *Ex parte Virginia*,[20] in which the concept of state action was more directly in issue. In the first case the Court refused to permit the removal of a criminal prosecution against a Negro from a state to a federal court under the Civil Rights Act of 1866, on the basis of the interpretation of that statute. But Justice Strong went beyond the necessities of the case to say that the Fourteenth Amendment and the Act of 1866 prohibited state action alone and that a mixed jury in a particular case was not essential to the requirement of equal protection. Although he employed expressions which implied that only positive state action was prohibited, his language was perhaps ambiguous, and certainly it did not resolve the issue.

In *Ex parte Virginia* the Court was confronted with the constitutional question of whether the action of a jury commissioner in excluding Negroes from juries and grand juries under a state law which permitted them to serve was state action, and therefore a denial of the Civil Rights Act of 1875, which levied fines not exceeding $5,000 on state officers excluding Negroes from jury service or failing to call them for it. Although there was no question concerning the validity of the Virginia laws, the Court held that the failure of the jury commissioner to call Negro jurors was state action, a denial of equal protection, and a violation of the Civil Rights Act of 1875, on the assumption that the state can act

[18] *Ibid.*, 306, 307–308.   [19] 100 U.S. 313 (1880).   [20] 100 U.S. 339 (1880).

only through its officials and that no agency of the state, its officers, or agents can deny to any person the equal protection of the laws. "Whoever, by virtue of public position under a state government, deprives another of property, life or liberty without due process of law, or denies or takes away the equal protection of the laws, violates the constitutional inhibition; and as he acts in the name [of] and for the State, and is clothed with the State's power, his act is that of the State." Similarly, supplementary legislation must act on persons and not "upon the abstract thing denominated a State." [21] In conclusion the Court sustained the validity of the fourth section of the Act of 1875 and answered the states'-rights arguments of Virginia and Justice Field by stating that the amendment created new rights, curbed state power, and expanded federal authority.

After 1878 no case came to the Court involving prosecution by the Department of Justice of state officials for illegal discrimination against Negroes in the selection of juries and grand juries. However, cases involving such discriminations continued to come to the Supreme Court on appeal from criminal convictions of Negroes in state courts where persons were disqualified from jury service either by state law or by failure of jury commissioners to call them. State laws disqualifying Negroes for jury service, though ingeniously drawn, were uniformly held unconstitutional in the earlier cases.[22] However, in most of the cases involving charges of official discrimination through maladministration of equal laws, the Court held that the absence of Negroes from juries or grand juries per se was not a denial of equal protection. The burden of proving discrimination because of race was placed upon the person convicted.[23]

[21] *Ibid.*, 347. For a recent treatment of the concept of state action see "State Action, A Study of Requirements under the Fourteenth Amendment," 1 *Race Relations Law Reporter*, 613 (1956).

[22] See, e.g., *Neal* v. *Delaware*, 103 U.S. 70 (1881); *Bush* v. *Kentucky*, 107 U.S. 110 (1883).

[23] *Wood* v. *Brush*, 140 U.S. 278 (1891); *Williams* v. *Mississippi*, 170 U.S. 213

To be sure, many of these cases presented the issues improperly and were inadequately argued, but the Court was hardly hospitable to Negroes challenging their exclusion from grand juries until 1935, when it had become more alert with respect to racial discrimination and the issues were adequately presented and competently argued in *Norris* v. *Alabama*.[24]

Contrary to the tenor of some of the jury cases, the Court rendered a notable opinion in *Yick Wo* v. *Hopkins*.[25] The case involved a San Francisco ordinance which prohibited the operation of laundries in wooden buildings without a permit from the board of supervisors, ostensibly with a view to reducing fire hazards. However, as the law was administered, two hundred Chinese were uniformly denied permits, and all but one of eighty occidentals were granted them. Although the Court regarded the ordinance as fair on its face, it declared it an unconstitutional denial of equal protection because of discriminations imposed through maladministration. In one of the more eloquent tributes to Western conceptions of freedom, Justice Stanley Matthews, speaking for a unanimous court, proclaimed that the nature and theory of American institutions leave no room "for the play and action of purely personal and arbitrary power," and that "the very idea that one man may be compelled to hold his life, or the means of living, or any material right essential to the enjoyment of life, at the mere will of another, seems to be intolerable in any country where freedom prevails, as being the essence of slavery itself." [26]

Accordingly, the facts as presented proved that the administration of the law was directed so exclusively against

---

(1898); *Tarrance* v. *Florida,* 188 U.S. 519 (1903); *Martin* v. *Texas,* 200 U.S. 316 (1906), and cases cited therein; *Thomas* v. *Texas,* 212 U.S. 278 (1909); *Franklin* v. *South Carolina,* 218 U.S. 161 (1910). See, however, *Rogers* v. *Alabama,* 192 U.S. 226 (1904), where discrimination was found in the exclusion of Negroes from jury service.
[24] 294 U.S. 587.   [25] 118 U.S. 356 (1886).   [26] *Ibid.,* 370.

a particular class of persons as to warrant the conclusion that, regardless of the intent of the ordinance, it was applied by public authorities representing the state "with a mind so unequal and oppressive" as to amount to a practical denial of equal protection. "Though the law itself be fair on its face and impartial in appearance, yet, if it is applied and administered by public authority with an evil eye and an unequal hand, so as practically to make unjust and illegal discriminations between persons in similar circumstances, material to their rights, the denial of equal justice is still within the prohibition of the Constitution." [27]

The last and one of the most important developments in judicial application of the equal protection clause in the nineteenth century was the emergence of the equal but separate formula in 1896 to sustain state laws compelling racial segregation in transportation, schools, and other public facilities, whether maintained by private owners or public authorities. Segregation by law played an insignificant role in the South prior to the Civil War, because custom and the concomitants of slavery were more than adequate in their own way to control race relations. Segregation laws, accordingly, were a northern import insofar as they were an outgrowth of the statutes of many northern states imposing serious disabilities on free Negroes as a class. In the face of

---

[27] *Ibid.*, 373–74. For cases distinguishing the Yick Wo decision see *Quong Wing* v. *Kirkendall*, 223 U.S. 59 (1912); *Ah Sin* v. *Wittman*, 198 U.S. 500 (1905). For cases involving statutes discriminating against aliens see *Frick* v. *Webb*, 263 U.S. 326 (1923); *Terrace* v. *Thompson*, 263 U.S. 197 (1923); *Webb* v. *O'Brien*, 263 U.S. 313 (1923); *Cockrill* v. *California*, 268 U.S. 258 (1925), all of which sustained restrictions on ownership of lands by aliens. See also *Patsone* v. *Pennsylvania*, 232 U.S. 138 (1914), which sustained a state statute prohibiting aliens from owning firearms and shooting wild game except in defense of person and property. On the other hand, the Court has almost uniformly invalidated state legislation restricting the employment of aliens by private enterprise. *Traux* v. *Raich*, 239 U.S. 33 (1915); *Heim* v. *McCall*, 239 U.S. 175 (1915). See, however, *Ohio* ex rel. *Clarke* v. *Deckenbach*, 274 U.S. 392 (1927), in which the Court sustained a Cincinnati ordinance disqualifying aliens from operating pool rooms, on the traditional assumption that pool halls are by nature centers of iniquity.

these onerous restrictions the emergence of separate public schools for Negroes in Boston and elsewhere was progress of great magnitude in a land where people were more and more coming to regard education as a means of secular salvation, for, prior to the establishment of separate schools for Negroes, they were barred from the public schools as a class, and obtained such meager education as they did wherever they found it. In the South free public school education of any kind rested on a most precarious base prior to the Civil War, and even afterwards, and legal efforts were made to prevent free Negroes from learning to read and write, lest they learn of abolitionist doctrine and spread subversive ideas among the slaves. Similarly, Negro preachers were suppressed, and after the war they met with serious discouragement. In religious matters, at least, the whites did not desire separate facilities and, paradoxically, the Negroes did, both for obvious reasons.

The establishment of separate Negro schools and of a firmer base for public education generally was a legacy respectively of the Freedmen's Bureau and the carpetbagger. After Reconstruction the southern states continued to provide meager support for public schools, partly in order to avert federal intervention and partly in order to provide vocational training and other skills for Negroes at a time when they had become so lazy, according to T. S. Stribling, that the whites were about to starve to death. General segregation by law in the South did not become important until the 1890's, when one southern legislature after another began to enact a wide variety of statutes compelling separation of the races. This was not in response to any spontaneous public demand, but because of the clamor of demagogues who endeavored to outdo each other in running for office against the Negro as a fictitious opponent. Their purpose was both to get into office and to suppress Populist ideas among poor whites by throwing them a crumb of consolation in the idea that independently of their wretched poverty they were white and thereby better than the Negro, who in the future would be kept "in his place" by law.[28]

The equal but separate formula originally was neither a constitutional provision nor a judicial gloss on the Constitution. The formula first came to the attention of the Supreme Court in *Louisville, N.O. & T. Ry.* v. *Mississippi*,[29] which involved a Mississippi statute requiring all passenger trains to provide "equal but separate facilities for the white and colored races." The Court sustained the measure on the ground that the act was not a regulation of interstate commerce and made no reference to equal protection.

It was not until six years later that the formula received judicial sanction in the face of the equal protection clause in *Plessy* v. *Ferguson*,[30] in which the Court sustained a Louisiana statute requiring railroads to provide "equal but separate" accommodations for white and colored passengers. In an opinion redolent with sociological speculation, permeated with theories of social Darwinism, and carrying overtones of white racial supremacy as scientific truth, Justice Henry Billings Brown, as spokesman for the Court, found the statute valid as imposing no involuntary servitude under the Thirteenth Amendment and no illegal discrimination under the Fourteenth. He declared: "A statute which implies merely a legal distinction between the white and colored races—a distinction which is founded in the color of the two races, and which must always exist so long as white men are distinguished

---

[28] On these issues see Paul Lewinson, *Race, Class and Party* (New York, 1932), 18; Charles S. Johnson, *Patterns of Negro Segregation* (New York, 1943), 159–61, 163–64; Gunnar Myrdal, *An American Dilemma* (New York, 1944), 579, note 2, 888; Milton R. Konvitz, *The Constitution and Civil Rights* (New York, 1947), 132–41; C. Vann Woodward, *The Strange Career of Jim Crow* (New York, 1955), *passim*. See also Wilbur J. Cash, *The Mind of the South* (New York, 1941). The discussion of the "equal but separate" formula is based largely on my article, "The Constitution, Education, and Segregation," 29 *Temple Law Quarterly* 409 (1956), 409–15.
[29] 133 U.S. 587 (1890).   [30] 163 U.S. 537 (1896).

from the other race by color—has no tendency to destroy the legal equality of the two races, or re-establish a state of involuntary servitude."

From this assumption, inconsistent within itself and contrary to the facts of social life, Justice Brown argued that although the purpose of the Fourteenth Amendment was "undoubtedly to enforce the absolute equality of the two races before the law," it could not have been intended in the nature of things "to abolish distinctions based upon color, or to enforce social, as distinguished from political, equality. . . ." Here Justice Brown distorted constitutional history and departed from earlier precedents. If there was one clear intention of the framers of the Fourteenth Amendment, it was to abolish all legal distinctions based on color and in no sense to enforce political equality except in a most indirect way. The reference to social equality is wholly irrelevant, for social equality, as Justice Harlan forcefully indicated in his dissent, is not produced merely because two people ride side by side in the same train or sit together in a jury box.

Segregation laws, Justice Brown continued with sociological confidence, "do not necessarily imply the inferiority of either race to the other," and are a reasonable exercise of the state's police power. He cited the existence of separate schools as the most common type of segregation and invoked as his principal authority for the validity of segregation the case of *Roberts* v. *City of Boston,*[31] in which Massachusetts' Chief Justice Lemuel Shaw rejected Charles Sumner's eloquent plea for equality before the law and sustained the power of the city of Boston to maintain separate schools for Negroes. The Roberts case, however, was hardly good authority. It antedated the Civil War and was repudiated by the Massachusetts legislature in 1855 in a statute prohibiting school segregation. After citing more relevant cases the

[31] 59 Mass. (5 Cush.) 198 (1849).

Justice returned to his distinction between laws "interfering with the political equality of the negro" and those requiring segregation of the races in public places. Moreover, the Court found that the validity of all such legislation depends on its reasonableness and, making another departure from previous cases and history, contended that the legislature, in determining reasonableness, "is at liberty to act with reference to the established usages, customs, and traditions of the people, and with a view to the promotion of their comfort, and the preservation of the public peace and good order." [32]

Justice Brown finally detected two fallacies in Plessy's argument. One was the assumption that segregation branded the Negro with a badge of inferiority, an assumption which could be true only because the colored race placed that interpretation on it. The other fallacy was the assumption that "social prejudices may be overcome by legislation, and that equal rights cannot be secured to the negro except by an enforced commingling of the two races." These arguments consist not only of dubious psychology in attributing inferiority exclusively to a state of mind, but also of poor logic in confusing the absence of segregation with the elimination of social prejudices and the enforced commingling of the races. Then, upon assumptions founded in social Darwinism, Justice Brown extolled the inefficacy of law as a means of social control of race relations by intoning: "Legislation is powerless to eradicate racial instincts or to abolish distinctions based upon physical differences, and the attempt to do so can only result in accentuating the difficulties of the present situation. If the civil and political rights of both races be equal, one cannot be inferior to the other civilly or politically. If one race be inferior to the other socially, the Constitution of the United States cannot put them upon the same plane." [33] Here Justice Brown's jurisprudence is no better than his history, sociology, or psychology. It may be

[32] *Plessy* v. *Ferguson,* 163 U.S. 537, 543, 544, 550.   [33] *Ibid.,* 551–52.

true, as the poet said, that "stone walls do not a prison make, nor iron bars a cage," but, supplemented by armed guards, they provide a very effective substitute. The fact is, of course, that laws do change customs and traditions even to the extent of uprooting them. Law and its penal sanctions have indeed changed the most stubborn of customs with respect to the legal status of Negroes.

The opinion of the Court in *Plessy* v. *Ferguson* is a compound of bad logic, bad history, bad sociology, and bad constitutional law. It ignored and ran counter to the history of the Civil Rights Act of 1866, the Freedmen's Bureau Act, the Fourteenth Amendment, and subsequent supplementary legislation, the firm purpose of all of which was to uproot unequal laws, customs, and traditions. It accepted uncritically either expressly or implicitly the vogue in social thinking in 1896 as reflected by theories of racial supremacy and social Darwinism. More important, it ran counter to the Court's own decisions from the Strauder case through the Civil Rights Cases.[34] Restrictive as some of the Court's earlier decisions were with respect to the scope of the Fourteenth Amendment, they all emphatically condemned every legal distinction based on race or color and enunciated absolute equality before the law. Even the decision in the Civil Rights Cases is clear on this issue. Here the Court struck down an act of Congress abolishing segregation in public conveyances, inns, and theaters, on the ground that it was discrimination, not by the states, but by private action, and left the clear implication that segregation as a form of state discrimination would be unconstitutional as a denial of the equal protection of the laws and certainly within the power of Congress to condemn.

Moreover, the decisions in the Civil Rights Cases and in some of its predecessors, limiting the scope of equal protection were reached out of a tender solicitude for the

[34] 109 U.S. 3 (1883).

maintenance of federalism. The decision in the Plessy case, although it sustained the validity of legislation, rested on laissez-faire assumptions with respect to governmental control of race relations. For the first time, too, it extended the rational basis test employed by the Court in disposing of equal protection issues in cases involving regulation and taxation to sustain racial discrimination. Prior to the Plessy case the Court uniformly regarded all racial discrimination perpetrated by a state or its agencies as invidious and void regardless of its alleged reasonableness. On the basis of every consideration, therefore, the decision in the Plessy case was a departure from precedents and was wrong when made. Hence, when it was reversed fifty-eight years later, it should have been overturned on that ground and no other.

In contrast to the opinion of the Court, Justice Harlan's dissent was characterized by sound logic, accurate history as far as it went, correct constitutional law, and, above all these, high moral assumptions and aspirations. He rejected the idea that in the eyes of the Constitution and the laws there can be a superior, dominant, or ruling class, and proclaimed: "Our Constitution is color blind and neither knows nor tolerates classes among citizens. In respect of civil rights all citizens are equal before the law." With prophetic accuracy he forecast that the decision would "stimulate aggressions, more or less brutal and irritating," on the rights of Negroes and defeat the purposes of the Civil War amendments.[35]

Although *Plessy* v. *Ferguson* was authoritative for fifty-eight years, and its rationale was extended to sustaining segregation in the public schools, subsequent judicial sanctions of it between 1896 and 1926 are hardly impressive. Certainly, *Cumming* v. *Board of Education* [36] was a frail support. There, all the Court did was to sustain the suspension of the sole Negro high school (containing sixty pupils) in a Georgia county so as to use its building for a

---

[35] *Plessy* v. *Ferguson*, 559–61.   [36] 175 U.S. 528 (1899).

Negro elementary school with three hundred pupils. Because three private high schools charging the same tuition fee as the Negro school were available to Negroes and because of the improper presentation of issues, Justice Harlan, as spokesman for a unanimous court, could find no evidence of racial discrimination. Moreover, the case did not in any way present the constitutional issue of segregated education. The same observations are true of *Gong Lum* v. *Rice*,[37] in which Gong Lum, a Chinese, challenged only the classification of his daughter as colored so as to exclude her from white schools in the absence of separate schools for Chinese. It is true that Chief Justice William Howard Taft, as was often his habit, went beyond the necessities of the case to affirm the validity of segregated education on the basis of the Roberts and Plessy cases, and thereby continued the uncritical analogy between schools and transportation. Indeed, it was not until 1938 in *Missouri* ex rel. *Gaines* v. *Canada* [38] that the equal but separate formula as applied to public education was given full acceptance by the Court, in a case directly presenting the issue. And this case, paradoxically, was the beginning of the end of racial segregation in the public schools.

Although judicial contraction of equal protection through the equal but separate formula reached its apex in the Plessy case, another phase of compulsory segregation is worthy of passing attention. In *Berea College* v. *Kentucky* [39] a private sectarian college dedicated to the Christian conception of equality and chartered to maintain an institution of higher learning "in order to promote the cause of Christ" admitted Negroes equally with whites and thereby ran afoul of an act of the Kentucky legislature, which had somewhat different notions of the Gospel according to St. Paul and of the Sermon on the Mount. Berea College was fined $1,000 for teaching Negroes in the same place simultaneously with whites, con-

[37] 275 U.S. 78 (1926).   [38] 305 U.S. 337 (1938).   [39] 211 U.S. 45 (1908).

trary to the provisions of the statute. The Supreme Court, in a seven-to-two decision, sustained the statute and the conviction on the rather narrow grounds that the law did not prohibit the college from teaching whites and Negroes at the same place at different times, and that the legislature which had chartered the college had the power to change its charter, something, of course, which had not been done. The decision evoked another thundering dissent from Justice Harlan, who, joined by Justice William R. Day, no longer stood in eccentric solitude. Justice Harlan emphasized the right to teach as a lawful calling and the right of white and colored persons to associate with each other in schools, churches, market places, and in public generally under the due process clause. He did give indirect approval to segregation in the public schools by declaring that his remarks in this context had "no reference to regulations prescribed for public schools, established at the pleasure of the state and maintained at the public expense." But he immediately added, "No such question is here presented and it need not now be discussed." [40]

In general the picture drawn by the decisions of the Court dealing with political equality under the Fifteenth Amendment and under the equal protection clause of the Fourteenth is not substantially different from that presented above. Due to that irony of judicial fate which has ensnared other amendments, it is somewhat strange that a significant number of the suffrage and elections cases have been decided on the basis of the equal protection clause, which was not designed at all to protect political rights, rather than the Fifteenth Amendment, which was so designed. In *United States* v. *Reese* [41] the Court invalidated two sections of the Enforcement Act of 1870 on the ground that they prohibited *all* interferences with the right of Negroes to vote rather than those based on race, color, or previous condition of servitude.

[40] *Ibid.,* 69.   [41] 92 U.S. 214 (1876).

The reasoning of the Court was similar to that in *United States* v. *Harris* [42] and the dicta in the Cruikshank case.[43] However, the Court did sustain federal power under the Enforcement Act to punish state election officials for violations of state law in the conduct of federal elections,[44] and to punish state election officers for refusing to count Negro votes and for making false returns, on the assumption that the right to have one's vote counted is as open to federal protection as the right to vote itself.[45]

The Court has also uniformly invalidated, under the Fifteenth Amendment, "grandfather clauses" in statutes, designed to exempt white persons from literacy tests. It has likewise invalidated other onerous registration requirements designed to prevent Negroes from voting for reasons other than race, color, or previous condition of servitude.[46] Similarly, it has condemned the device of the white primary as a denial of equal protection when established directly by statute or indirectly through legislative authorization.[47] In general the suffrage and elections cases left the states with considerable discretion to prevent Negroes from voting, so long as they either did not base exclusion from the suffrage on overt grounds of race or, if they did, disguised it with that genteel prudence characteristic of southern legal genius in the latter part of the nineteenth and the early part of the twentieth century.

Judicial interpretation of the equal protection clause between the ratification of the Fourteenth Amendment and 1935 is characterized by five major developments. The first,

[42] 106 U.S. 629 (1883).   [43] *United States* v. *Cruikshank*, 92 U.S. 542 (1876).
[44] *Ex parte Siebold*, 100 U.S. 371 (1880).
[45] *United States* v. *Mosley*, 238 U.S. 383 (1915).
[46] *Guinn* v. *United States*, 238 U.S. 347 (1915); *Myers* v. *Anderson*, 238 U.S. 368 (1915). For a later case see *Lane* v. *Wilson*, 307 U.S. 268 (1939).
[47] *Nixon* v. *Herndon*, 273 U.S. 536 (1927); *Nixon* v. *Condon*, 286 U.S. 73 (1932), only to sustain the white primary later, when decreed by a state Democratic convention, on the fiction, since repudiated, that a political party is a mere private club and its actions are not state action. *Grovey* v. *Townsend*, 295 U.S. 45 (1935); reversed in *Smith* v. *Allwright*, 321 U.S. 649 (1944).

though not necessarily the first in chronology, was the extension of the clause so as to provide a somewhat feeble protection to economic interests and the property rights of corporations as well as natural persons. Although the framers of the amendment do not appear to have had such an application in mind, the text of the equal protection clause certainly did not preclude such a construction. Second, the Court narrowly confined the scope of congressional power to enforce the clause in the fifth section, limiting that power to the enactment of remedial legislation corrective of unequal state laws, customs and practices, and discriminatory action by officials acting under color of state authority. Neither the historical background nor the text of the amendment appears to justify such an interpretation or such a narrow conception of state action. The weight of all the evidence is that the amendment was designed not only to condemn all partial and unequal laws of the states with respect to the Negro, but also to authorize Congress to exercise a secondary power to protect the Negro and other persons against private oppressions in the event of failure of the states to do so in their exercise of a primary responsibility. Third, despite other restrictive interpretations, the Court, except in *Plessy* v. *Ferguson,* emphatically condemned all legal discriminations based on race or color as a consequence of its conception of the amendment as establishing absolute equality before the law. Fourth, the Court was equally emphatic in applying the principle of equality before the law so as unequivocally to condemn unequal and partial administration of laws fair on their face and otherwise valid. Fifth, it made a second notable contraction of the amendment when it sanctioned segregation through an oblique and tacit acceptance of the equal but separate formula.

Prior to 1935 approximately the only benefit obtained by the Negro was the right, more juridical than real, to be free from racial discrimination in the selection of juries and occasionally to be free from discrimination in state election and suffrage laws. Many of these cases, to be sure, were most poorly prepared and presented by counsel, and some even presented issues in the wrong way. However, there is no evidence to support a belief that the Court's decisions would have been different in any other situation. It is perhaps significant that the two most restrictive decisions provoked vigorous dissents which could become the basis for subsequent reversals in different times and conditions.

By 1900 the elaborate apparatus for the enforcement of equal rights in the Civil Rights Act of 1866, the Fourteenth and Fifteenth amendments, and subsequent legislation of 1870, 1871, and 1875 was largely a failure, and continued in a somewhat less degree to be so in 1959. As the dour Thad Stevens had bitterly forecast, the day came when Democratic majorities in Congress, supported by a Democratic President, repealed substantial portions of the legislation. Even Republicans displayed a chronic indifference to racial discriminations except during election campaigns, when their interest became acute. Indifferent and inactive Presidents and disinterested or timid Attorneys General did little to enforce the amendments and the remnants of the statutes; and the Supreme Court, as we have seen, imposed very considerable obstacles by invalidating key provisions of federal statutes and construing others and the amendments strictly.

The net effect of all these cases was to make the Supreme Court, and not Congress, the major organ for the enforcement of the Fourteenth Amendment, contrary to the expectations of its framers and the clear meaning of its text. The transfer of power from Congress to the Court was a major constitutional defeat for the Radical Republicans, who were thereby deprived of the fruits of their political victories, and it was, in turn, a major triumph for the South, which was given a free hand in the control of race relations so long as southern states refrained from making or enforcing laws in an unequal, hostile, and oppressive manner. Although the South had lost the war, it had conquered constitutional law. Regardless of any subsequent developments in constitutional interpretation, the Court had emerged as an ally of the South in a most critical period of its existence as a conscious sectional minority. In turn, it was inevitable that what the South did with this constitutional victory, and how the southern states used the powers taken from them by constitutional amendment and restored to them by judicial decision, would inexorably influence the future course of judicial interpretation. It is melancholy to record that the southern states, instead of using their newly restored powers over race relations to bring about a gradual improvement of the legal, political, and economic status of Negroes, used them in a discriminatory and oppressive manner, with a view to keeping the colored race in a low, servile, and cringing status, under the leadership of irresponsible office seekers who fanned the flames of racial hatred and rode into office on the back of the Negro.

CHAPTER FIVE

The Court Returns
to the Constitution

JUST WHEN THE COURT BEGAN ITS
slow and still partial return to the Constitution is a matter
of conjecture, but one may date it roughly in 1935, when it
began to subject racial discrimination in the selection of
trial and grand juries to careful scrutiny, or even as early as
1932, when it began a continuing insistence on fair trial
procedure for Negroes and other members of submerged
groups accused of crime.[1] In any event, the transformation
of judicial attitudes toward Negro rights was begun by a
conservative Court well before the constitutional revolution
of 1937.

Whatever the date, the factors contributing to the Court's
change in approach are more important. The great de-
pression and the measures taken to ameliorate it were levellers of a kind, and the war against Nazi Germany and its
racist dogmas, with preachments of equality by American
leaders, was a great equalizer. Beyond these forces, however,
was the rise of the Negro race economically and politically
to the extent that more Negroes were ready to challenge

[1] *Powell* v. *Alabama,* 287 U.S. 45 (1932).

discriminations which in other times were accepted with indifference or resignation. Finally, by 1935 powerful groups, well supported by numbers and money, had arisen to work for the cause of Negroes in the civil rights vineyard, so that the cases presented in the 1930's and afterwards were, for the most part, based on adequately prepared records in the trial court and were always marked by the most competent presentation of issues in appellate proceedings, in startling contrast to the improper presentation of issues and the inadequate preparation of arguments so characteristic of earlier cases.[2]

Despite sporadic judicial condemnations of discrimination against Negroes in the selection of juries and grand juries between 1880 and 1935 and frequent disapprovals since 1935, jury officials continued to persist in systematic and flagrant violations of the federal Constitution, either out of ignorance of the decisions of the Supreme Court or in deliberate defiance of them. It is no surprise, therefore, that the jury cases constitute the largest single category of litigation involving equal protection which has appeared before the Supreme Court in its contemporary history, or since 1935. The repetition of such discrimination and the frequent recurrence of cases involving it are testimony both of greater judicial vigilance with regard to constitutional rights and of the inefficacy of judicial action in itself, unsupplemented by legislative and executive intervention, to obtain the broad objective of equality before the law.

However, in spite of the relative inefficacy of decisions condemning discrimination in the selection of juries, greater concern by the Court for the preservation of equality before the law in this area has at least prevented miscarriages of justice in specific cases as a result of racial discrimination.

[2] For the role of the National Association for the Advancement of Colored People in some of these cases, see Clement E. Vose, *Caucasians Only: The Supreme Court, the N.A.A.C.P., and Restrictive Covenants* (Berkeley, 1959).

More alertness to racial discrimination was first shown by the Court in the contemporary history of equal protection in *Norris v. Alabama*,[3] one of the so-called Scottsboro cases, which collectively constitute a landmark in the development of safeguards for persons charged with criminal offenses. In the Norris case the record showed that in Jackson County, Alabama, with a total population of 36,881 in 1930, of whom 2,688 were Negroes, no Negro had served on a grand or petty jury within the memory of living witnesses, and for the years 1930–1931 the names of only six Negroes were on the jury rolls and were designated by red lines. Likewise, it was the practice to designate Negroes on the jury roll with the abbreviation "col." In Morgan County, where the case was tried after a change in venue, the population in 1930 was 46,176, including 8,311 Negroes. Again no Negro had been called for jury service in that county within the memory of living witnesses. There was evidence to show that many Negroes possessed the qualifications of jurors, but none was even placed on the jury rolls. Despite denials by state and local authorities of conscious discrimination against Negroes, the Supreme Court found a "long-continued, unvarying, and wholesale exclusion of Negroes from jury service" inconsistent with the constitutional mandate of equal protection.

Subsequent cases present a similar picture of wholesale exclusion of Negroes from jury service. In St. John the Baptist Parish, Louisiana, with a Negro population of almost 50 per cent, of whom at least 70 per cent were literate, no Negro had served on a jury between 1896 and 1936. Moreover, a venire of three hundred in December, 1936, contained the names of only three Negroes, one of whom was dead, and another of whom was called for jury service in 1937—the only one so called within the memory of the sheriff, the clerk of court, or any other witnesses.[4] Although

[3] 294 U.S. 587 (1935).   [4] *Pierre v. Louisiana*, 306 U.S. 354 (1939).

a few Negroes had been called for jury service in Harris
County, Texas, between 1931 and 1938, they were a rarity,
and the Supreme Court found prima facie evidence of the
deliberate exclusion of Negroes as a class from jury service
in that county.[5] Similar patterns of illegal discrimination
have been found to be denials of equal protection in Lauder-
dale County, Mississippi; Dallas County, Texas; Jackson
County, Texas (against Mexicans); and Cobb County,
Georgia.[6] In all of these situations, which involved the
criminal conviction of Negroes by all-white juries, the
Supreme Court reversed the convictions as inconsistent with
the requirements of equal protection, on the theory as once
stated by Justice Black that "equal protection to all is the
basic principle upon which justice under the law rests."[7]

With such frequent reversals of convictions of Negroes by
all-white juries, it was inevitable that legal devices designed
to meet the requirements of formal constitutionality would
be contrived by jury officials having even a vicarious knowledge of Supreme Court decisions. Hence, jury officials in
Fulton County, Georgia, devised a scheme for placing the
names of white veniremen on white cards and of Negroes on
yellow cards, without any authorization by statute. Although
Negroes comprised 25 per cent of Fulton County's population in 1950, 14 per cent of the tax receiver's digest, and 5
per cent of the jury list, no Negro was on the panel of
sixty jurors from which a jury was selected to try a Negro
indicted for rape. A majority of the Court, speaking by
Chief Justice Fred Vinson, found the use of the colored
cards prima facie evidence of discrimination because it provided opportunity for discrimination. Even Justice Stanley

[5] *Smith* v. *Texas,* 311 U.S. 128 (1940). See also *Hill* v. *Texas,* 316 U.S. 400 (1942).
[6] *Patton* v. *Mississippi,* 332 U.S. 463 (1947); *Cassell* v. *Texas,* 339 U.S. 282 (1950);
    Hernandez v. *Texas,* 347 U.S. 475 (1954); *Reece* v. *Georgia,* 350 U.S. 85
    (1955). See also *Hale* v. *Kentucky,* 303 U.S. 613 (1938); *Shephard* v. *Florida,*
    341 U.S. 50 (1951).
[7] *Pierre* v. *Louisiana,* 306 U.S. 354, 358 (1939).

Reed, a frequent dissenter in such cases, concurred in the judgment, but on the basis of the census. Justice Frankfurter also pointed to opportunities for discrimination in the use of colored cards and noted the startling result of their use, to conclude: "The mind of justice, not merely its eyes, would have to be blind to attribute such an occurrence to mere fortuity." [8]

There have been, of course, a few deviations from the even tenor of the Court's way in jury cases since 1935. In *Akins* v. *Texas* [9] it held that equal protection does not require proportional representation of Negroes on grand juries in the absence of a clear showing of systematic discrimination. Because the Negro population of Dallas County at the time was only 15½ per cent of the total, a proportion which would have entitled Negroes to 1.8552 jurors of every 12, independently of qualifications, and because of conflicting evidence concerning discrimination, the Court found no denial of equal protection. Chief Justice Stone and Justice Black dissented in silence. Justice Murphy dissented vigorously and Justice Rutledge concurred in the result. Although the decision can be taken to mean that in this particular case the Court was satisfied with token compliance, the close division of the Court and Justice Reed's carefully guarded language do not warrant such a conclusion.

The issue of proportional representation on juries was later presented in *Brown* v. *Allen*,[10] in which the Court sustained the practice of jury officials in Forsyth County, North Carolina, of compiling jury rolls from poll and personalty lists of taxpayers. In this county Negroes accounted for 32.5 per cent of the population and 16 per cent of the taxpayers in 1940. In 1949–1950 the number of Negroes on grand jury panels ranged from 7 to 10 per cent and in 1950,

[8] *Avery* v. *Georgia*, 345 U.S. 559, 564 (1953). See also *Williams* v. *Georgia*, 349 U.S. 375 (1955).
[9] 325 U.S. 398 (1945).   [10] 344 U.S. 469 (1953).

on petty jury panels, they ranged from 9 to 17 per cent. Because no discrimination was found in the drawing of names from the jury box, the Court, speaking by Justice Reed, was unwilling to interfere with what it regarded as a lawful method for the compilation of jury panels, even though it admitted that the tax rolls had a higher percentage of white citizens than colored, "doubtless due to inequality of educational and economic opportunities." [11] This admission is probably more significant than the decision, in that it recognizes that inequalities are progressive because their existence in one area perpetuates them in others, even in those involving constitutional rights, a fact which did not escape the notice of Justice Black, joined by Justice Douglas in dissent.

The Akins and Brown decisions, taken in connection with the two New York cases sustaining New York's "blue ribbon" jury system in the absence of a showing of racial discrimination,[12] suggest methods for excluding Negroes from jury service on grounds other than race and reflect a rather serious respect of the Court for local self-determination in devising methods for the selection of juries. This same respect for state procedures is evident in *Michel* v. *Louisiana*,[13] in which the Court sustained the conviction of three Negroes in New Orleans, in the face of allegations of systematic exclusion of Negroes from jury service in a parish where the Negro population was 32 per cent of the total and where only one Negro, who appeared to be white and was so mistaken, had served on a jury within the memory of local witnesses. However, because objections to the composition of the trial jury were not made before the end of the third judicial day following the end of the grand jury's term, as required by statute, the Court refused to consider the issue, over the

[11] *Ibid.*, 467–70, 473.
[12] *Fay* v. *New York*, 322 U.S. 361 (1947); *Moore* v. *New York*, 332 U.S. 56 (1948). The second case involved the conviction of Negroes by an all-white jury.
[13] 350 U.S. 91 (1955).

protests of Justice Black, Chief Justice Warren, and Justice Douglas.

Despite occasional judicial deviations from a straight path of equal protection in the name of federalism or states' rights, the decisions involving the exclusion of Negroes from juries are very important. To be sure, they do not add much to the law as it was applied in 1880 in the Strauder case, but they do mark a change in the approach of the Supreme Court induced both by changes in general opinion favorable to equality before the law and by a better presentation of issues and preparation of cases by counsel representing Negroes. In this respect the emergence of the National Association for the Advancement of Colored People and the American Civil Liberties Union as major organs for the protection of constitutional rights in criminal cases are events of very great significance. In many of these cases these organizations provided skilled and astute attorneys to prepare briefs and arguments on appeal to the Supreme Court. In some of them "Yankee" and Negro lawyers appeared, dressed in "store-bought" clothes, to represent clients at the trial level in the rancid air and stale odors characteristic of many American county courthouses in all sections of the country. The extent to which these decisions actually protect Negroes accused of crime is a matter of conjecture, but little as it probably is, it marks a beginning.

From the standpoint of their contributions to constitutional development, the decisions dealing with restrictive covenants and the suffrage, though less numerous, are much more important than the jury cases because they enlarge significantly the concept of state action, in contrast to its earlier rather technical and rigidly narrow interpretation. As early as 1917 the Supreme Court invalidated a Louisville ordinance preventing white or colored persons from moving into blocks of residences inhabited preponderantly by the other, in the face of contentions that compulsory separation of the races in order to maintain racial purity, preserve property values from deterioration, and prevent racial conflicts was a valid exercise of the police power.[14] Although the Court used equal protection arguments from the Civil Rights Act of 1866 and from its early interpretations of the Fourteenth Amendment to denounce the ordinance as a drastic interdiction "based wholly upon color," the case really turned on the right of a white owner to sell his property to whomever he pleased under due process of law. As a result of this decision and of the earlier absences of state or local regulations on the subject, the device of restrictive covenants in deeds conveying real estate, whereby purchasers agreed never to sell to Negroes, Jews, or other racial or religious minorities, became commonplace throughout the country and received judicial sanction in *Corrigan* v. *Buckley*.[15] The nature of judicial proceedings as state action to enforce restrictive covenants was neither noticed nor argued.

This issue was presented in *Shelley* v. *Kraemer*,[16] where it was elaborately argued by both sides and where the NAACP played an especially important role, aided by the Department of Justice, the Civil Rights Department of the Grand Lodge of Elks, the National Lawyers Guild, the American Jewish Congress, the American Veterans Committee, the American Jewish Committee, the American Unitarian Association, and the American Association of the United Nations, among others. With three justices not participating, a unanimous court, speaking by Chief Justice Vinson, ruled that judicial enforcement of restrictive covenants designed to exclude persons as inhabitants of residential areas on the basis of race or color is state action and, as such, a denial of equal protection. The Court thereby made constitutional history. Chief Justice

[14] *Buchanan* v. *Warley*, 245 U.S. 60 (1917).   [15] 271 U.S. 323 (1926).
[16] 334 U.S. 1 (1948).

Vinson reviewed the early jury decisions and the Civil Rights Cases, which condemned all state discrimination "in the shape of laws, customs, or judicial or executive proceedings" and cited the Civil Rights Act of 1866, as carried over into the United States Code, which guaranteed the right of all citizens to enjoy the same rights as white citizens "to inherit, purchase, lease, sell, hold, and convey real and personal property." [17] On the basis of these and other authorities the Court found all judicial proceedings to be state action, while leaving undisturbed the covenants themselves, which it continued to regard as private action.

Because the suits in the Shelley case arose out of actions to evict Negroes from homes purchased by them in St. Louis and Detroit, the judgments of the state courts operated directly on them in a discriminatory manner. The decision, therefore, left unsettled the question of whether state courts could award damages in civil actions brought against a white owner for selling property to Negroes or Mongolians, contrary to land covenants, without at the same time disturbing the rights of colored persons to continue in their possession and occupancy of residential property. This issue was presented five years later in *Barrows* v. *Jackson*.[18] Justice Sherman Minton, as spokesman for the Court, reasoned that for a state court to compel a defendant to respond for damages would be to punish him for failure to discriminate against a non-Caucasian and, to that extent, to put its sanction behind the covenants, thereby replacing the respondent's voluntary choice with that of the state, so as to deny the equal protection of the laws. Chief Justice Vinson protested, in a solitary dissent, that insofar as the Shelley case did not affect the rights of private parties to enter into restrictive covenants based on race, and no non-Caucasian was injured or threatened with injury by the suit in question,

[17] Section 42, 8 U.S.C.A.   [18] 346 U.S. 249 (1953).

there was no jurisdiction to review and, on the merits of the case, no denial of equal protection.[19]

Although these cases reverse no previous decision employing the concept of state action, they are important as presenting a new judicial mentality. By leaving the covenants themselves undisturbed, they do raise questions as to whether their restrictions still common to all sections of the Republic are denials of equal protection when enforced by custom, social pressure, and economic or other sanctions. If the Court means all that it said in its invocation of the Civil Rights Act, and if that statute means what it says, it would be just a short step to declare that racially restrictive covenants are void per se wherever they are effective, or that the failure of the states to condemn them as contrary to public policy is inhibited state action. Any ruling to this effect would necessarily involve a shift of the Court's emphasis on state action from the nature of the organ or agent performing a function to the function itself and to its effect. However, such a shift has already been made in the cases involving primary elections and the role of political parties and other groups in the electoral process.

For that reason the decisions dealing with the right of Negroes to vote in primaries constitute a most important development in the interpretation of state action and, in turn, of equal protection. Notice has already been taken of how Texas, an experimental laboratory for conducting tests in the use of the white primary, after two judicial rebuffs and a helpful suggestion, probably unintended as such, from Justice Benjamin Cardozo, devised a temporarily successful white primary by doing nothing itself and leaving the

[19] For another restrictive covenant case see *Hurd* v. *Hodge*, 334 U.S. 24 (1948), in which the Court invalidated the enforcement of racial restrictions in a deed to property in the District of Columbia as a violation of the Civil Rights Act of 1866 rather than the due process clause of the Fifth Amendment. See also *Rice* v. *Sioux City Memorial Park*, 349 U.S. 70 (1954), involving the burial of a Winnebago Indian killed in the Korean War in a cemetery where lots were sold under racially restrictive covenants.

determination of party membership to the state party convention. The rationale of this procedure was the dual fiction
that political parties are private clubs for the pursuit of
private aims (even merriment) or other nongovernmental
ends, and that primaries are not a part of elections, even in a
state where the party nomination is tantamount to election.

In *United States* v. *Classic*,[20] which had nothing to do with
Negroes, the Court examined and thereby destroyed the
fiction that a nominating primary is not a part of an election,
and ruled that a corrupt New Orleans election official was
subject to the federal election laws for frauds committed in
counting the votes in a Democratic primary for the nomination of a candidate for Congress. The majority of the Court
emphasized both the nature of party primaries as an integral
part of an election under Louisiana law and the practical
effect of a Democratic nomination in a state where, his-
torically, if Republicans presented candidates at all, they did
so in a spirit of heroic futility as a ceremonial observance
of the mythical ideal of the Republican party as a national
party. In this important decision Justice Owen Roberts,
who had written the opinion of the Court in *Grovey* v.
Townsend,[21] was with the majority and, paradoxically, Justice Douglas dissented on statutory grounds. Justices Black
and Murphy supported his opinion. The alignment of the
Court suggests that the prediction of individual votes of
judges in specific cases is a hazardous enterprise.

Three years later, in *Smith* v. *Allwright*,[22] the superstition
that political parties are private associations dissociated from
government was given a deserved repose. In a majority
opinion by Justice Reed the Court invalidated the rule of
the Democratic convention of Texas excluding Negroes from
membership in the Democratic party, and thereby from
voting in Democratic primaries, and reversed *Grovey* v.
Townsend. Citing the Classic case and a complex network

[20] 313 U.S. 299 (1941).   [21] 295 U.S. 45.   [22] 321 U.S. 649 (1944).

of Texas statutes and regulations authorizing parties to conduct primaries, the Court found the conduct of a primary by the Democratic party to be state action within the meaning of the equal protection clause, and the exclusion of Negroes from primaries to be a violation of the Fifteenth Amendment. Justice Roberts was understandably grieved at this destruction of his handiwork in *Grovey* v. *Townsend,* and he wailed with some exaggeration that the decision overruling the Grovey case tended "to bring adjudications of this tribunal into the same class as a restricted railroad ticket, good for this day and train only." [23]

The decision in the Allwright case naturally produced consternation among those who would exclude all Negroes from voting regardless of the price. Hence they proceeded to devise schemes, as earlier generations had done, to evade constitutional requirements by legal means. But the generation of southern lawyers and politicians after the 1940's, with a few exceptions, lacked both the legal acumen and the political skills of their ancestors, who generally confined themselves to matching wits with their adversaries, whereas their successors butted heads against immovable walls. To be sure, the task of the later generation was greater than that of its precursors, in view of changed public opinion, judicial attitudes, and less anemia in the federal government, and this was serious enough. But added to this handicap was this group's considerable brevity of legal talents and political astuteness after 1945 in the area of race relations. It is no exaggeration, therefore, to conclude that its efforts were constitutionally doomed from the beginning.

One of the first efforts was the repeal by the legislature of South Carolina and other states of all legislation affecting political parties and primary elections, in the hope of restoring the fiction that parties are private clubs, in the face of

[23] *Ibid.,* 669.

Justice Frankfurter's earlier warning that the Fourteenth Amendment "nullifies sophisticated as well as simple-minded modes of discrimination." [24] In *Rice* v. *Elmore* [25] the Fourth Circuit Court of Appeals certainly did not regard South Carolina's repeal of party and primary laws as sophisticated, and persisted in calling the action of the Democratic party the action of the state. The Supreme Court left this decision undisturbed by denying review on certiorari.

A less simple-minded, more complicated, and equally unsuccessful form of discrimination was challenged in *Terry* v. *Adams*.[26] In 1889 the Jaybird Democratic Association was organized in Fort Bend County, Texas, with a membership consisting of the entire white voting population of the county as shown by the poll lists. For sixty years the Jaybirds conducted preprimary elections to endorse candidates for the Democratic nomination, independently of state law and at the expense of the association. During the sixty years of the association's existence, every person nominated for county office had obtained its endorsement, and, as a general rule, aspirants not endorsed by the Jaybirds rarely filed as candidates in the Democratic primary. In multiple opinions eight of the justices found the practice of the Jaybirds in excluding Negroes on the basis of race and color a violation of the Fifteenth Amendment, for three different sets of reasons.

Justice Black, joined by Justices Douglas and Harold Burton, following *Rice* v. *Elmore,* found the Jaybirds to be more than a private club and their function, on the basis of its effect and nature, to be state action. Justice Frankfurter looked beyond the thin veneer of state action and stressed both (1) the effect of endorsement by the Jaybirds and (2) the condoning of their practices, first by local officials clothed with state power, and, secondly, by the state in its failure to

[24] *Lane* v. *Wilson,* 307 U.S. 268, 275 (1939).
[25] 165 F.2d 387 (1947); 333 U.S. 875 (1948).   [26] 345 U.S. 461 (1953).

condemn the discrimination. Implicit in Justice Frankfurter's opinion are the ideas that the character of an act as state action is determined by its purpose and effect and that the failure of the state to condemn discriminatory practices touching on governmental functions is a denial of rights under the Fifteenth Amendment and, for that matter, under the Fourteenth. In other words, what the state permits, it commands, or, in the view of the framers of the Fourteenth and Fifteenth Amendments, acts of omission can be denials of constitutional rights as well as positive actions of legislatures, executives, and courts. Justice Clark, joined by Chief Justice Vinson and Justice Reed, formed a neutral core to argue that the Jaybird Association was a political party inseparable from the Democratic party, and that its activities fell within the self-executing ban of the Fifteenth Amendment. Justice Clark, like Justices Black and Frankfurter, stressed the effects of the Jaybirds' activities.

Central to all of the divergent opinions were the concepts of function and effect rather than the official or private nature of the organ, association, or agent engaged in the activity concerned. In this sense the multiple opinions in *Terry* v. *Adams* can mean that to the extent the concept of state action remains in constitutional jargon, it includes all functions of a public nature, even when performed by private organizations, groups, or agents. In that situation educational institutions, whether maintained and operated by a state or its subdivisions or by private corporations or associations, may be regarded as engaged in state action, and all racial discriminations by any of them, therefore, may be regarded as denials of equal protection.

Whether this conclusion with respect to education is clearly justified is certainly arguable in the light of the ambiguous *per curiam* opinion in the first Girard College case,[27] and possibly unwarranted by the Court's denial of

[27] *Pennsylvania* v. *Board of Directors of City Trusts*, 353 U.S. 230 (1957).

certiorari in the second.[28] Nevertheless, the decisions in the primary cases point in that direction and even toward a tendency to abandon the distinction between state and private action. In either situation the decisions in the primary cases represent one of the longest steps the Court has taken in its return to the Constitution as envisaged by the framers of the Fourteenth Amendment and by Justice Harlan in his polemical way in the Civil Rights Cases.

Just as the decisions of the Supreme Court in the jury cases have not banished all discriminations based on race or color in the compilation of jury lists, the decisions in the election cases have hardly eliminated the systematic exclusion of Negroes from the suffrage in wide areas of the South. As a result of violence, social and economic pressure, long and complicated registration forms and questionnaires, changing of registrar's office hours without notice, and fortuitous but temporary resignations of registration officials, not to mention outright refusal of registrars to enroll Negroes, the number of Negro registrants in the South has remained small. In 1959 Mr. Ralph McGill, relying on reports made by the Southern Regional Council, estimated that Negro registration in eleven southern states had reached a total of only 1,321,731, or approximately 25 per cent of the 4,980,000 Negroes of voting age.[29] Mississippi had the lowest rate,

---

[28] *Alker* v. *Girard Trust Corn Exchange Bank,* 358 U.S. 825, 901 (1958). The disposition of the first case by reference to *Brown* v. *Topeka Board of Education,* 347 U.S. 483 (1954), was unsatisfactory in that it did not meet the issue of state action in the exclusion of a Negro from a private school financed by a trust established by Stephen Girard for the education of white male orphans. The Girard trust was then administered by the Board of Directors of City Trusts, an organ of the city of Philadelphia. Subsequently the administration of the trust was transferred to a private trustee in order to carry out Girard's will to the letter. In denying certiorari the Court hardly clarified the issue in the first case, but did leave the inference that state action was involved in the first case and not in the second because of the nature of the trustee.

[29] The states are: Alabama, Arkansas, Florida, Georgia, Louisiana, Mississippi, North Carolina, South Carolina, Tennessee, Texas, and Virginia.

with only 30,000 to 35,000 Negroes enrolled to vote, of an adult Negro population of 500,000.[30] A vast increase in Negro voting had occurred in the cities within the fifteen years between 1944 and 1959, and some of this increase could be attributed directly to *Smith* v. *Allwright* and its successors. The Southern Regional Council has estimated that 80 to 85 per cent of the Negro vote in the South is in the cities or larger towns.[31] Thus in Atlanta and Nashville approximately as many Negroes vote as whites in proportion to the total population.

In other southern cities the picture is different, as in Montgomery, where a Negro, it is reported, votes only after something of an endurance contest with election officials. In the rural areas the pattern varies from county to county. Sworn testimony of registrars in Lowndes County, Alabama, before the Civil Rights Commission revealed not only that no Negro is enrolled to vote in that county, where the Negroes outnumber the whites four to one, but that no Negro has ever even tried to vote. Another extreme case is Macon County, Alabama, and the town of Tuskegee, where Negroes account for 84.4 per cent of the population, but where only 1,100 Negroes, less than 8 per cent of the Negro population, have registered to vote, leaving 13,000 or more unregistered Negroes of twenty-one years of age or older. The Macon County Negroes are somewhat different from those in Lowndes County. Many are middle class in terms of annual incomes of more than $5,000 for 4.5 per cent of all salaried workers and wage earners. Likewise, they are literate, even more so than the whites, because the Negroes on the faculty of Tuskegee Institute form the best educated class in the county. Moreover, 20 per cent of Tuskegee's Negroes who are twenty-five years of age or older have at least a high

---

[30] Ralph McGill, "If the Southern Negro Got the Vote," *New York Times Magazine* (June 21, 1959), 22.
[31] *Ibid.*

school education, more than twice the ratio of any other Alabama county.[32]

Such situations, aside from the special conditions in Tuskegee, are common throughout the rural South and in small towns. Evidence of such conditions and the truculence of Alabama election officials before the Civil Rights Commission in 1959 hardly support the contentions of southern senators and representatives in Congress that no voting discriminations exist in the South and that strengthening of federal election laws is unnecessary.

In view of widespread practices of excluding Negroes from voting, it is hardly surprising that the Negro has turned to Washington and that Congress has responded with the Civil Rights Act of 1957, the first such federal legislation since 1875.[33] Congress has since enacted the Civil Rights Act of 1960. Nor is it surprising that more demands are being made. Accordingly, southern recalcitrance on the part of prominent politicians, officials, and the county-seat elite with respect to Negro registration and voting may well intensify the South's problems at a critical period in its history. The bitter-end and last-ditch leaders of white resistance to federal authority, therefore, may be doing more in their way to advance the cause of racial equality than all the combined forces of the National Association for the Advancement of Colored People and its allies both North and South.

Two important developments affecting congressional power to enforce the Fourteenth Amendment were (1) the decisions in *United States* v. *Classic*[34] and *Screws* v. *United States*,[35] which resuscitated the second section of the Civil Rights Act of 1866 as carried over into Section 20 of the United States Criminal Code,[36] and (2) the decisions in a number of inter-

---

[32] Douglass Cater, "The Bitter Fruits of Southern Bitter Endism," *The Reporter*, XX (January 22, 1959), 27–31.
[33] 71 Stat. 634.   [34] 313 U.S. 299 (1941).
[35] 325 U.S. 91 (1945).   [36] Section 52, 18 U.S.C.A.

state transportation cases, which condemned segregation in public conveyances in interstate commerce under that provision of the Interstate Commerce Act of 1887 which forbids any discrimination by interstate carriers against any person whatsoever.

Long before these developments, however, the Court had held in *Truax* v. *Corrigan* [37] that due process and equal protection require a minimum of positive protection by the states, in the course of invalidating an Arizona statute designed primarily to forbid the issuance of injunctions by state courts to restrain peaceful picketing and the boycott. Speaking for himself and four other judges in the face of powerful dissents, Chief Justice Taft declared that due process "requires that every man shall have the protection of his day in court, and the benefit of the general law." Due process, he also asserted, "tends to secure equality of law in the sense that it makes a required minimum of protection for everyone's right of life, liberty, and property, which the Congress or the legislature may not withhold." [38] Then, turning to equal protection, he pointed to it as a guaranty against undue favor or class privilege and hostile discrimination or oppressive inequality, and declared that "the guaranty was intended to secure equality of protection not only for all, but against all similarly situated." [39]

In the Classic case the Court applied Sections 19 and 20 of the federal Criminal Code to ballot-box frauds in New Orleans, as noted earlier in another context. Section 19, a derivative of the Enforcement Act of 1870, makes it a crime to conspire to injure or oppress any citizen "in the free exercise of any right or privilege secured to him by the Constitution." Section 20 was construed so as to define two separate offenses: (1) willfully subjecting any inhabitant to the deprivation of rights secured by the Constitution under color of any law or custom, and (2) willfully subjecting any

[37] 257 U.S. 312 (1921).   [38] *Ibid.,* 332.   [39] *Ibid.,* 333.

inhabitant to different punishments because of alienage, color, or race than are prescribed for white citizens. The application of these statutes to the miscounting of votes and the certification of false returns sustains a broad power on the part of Congress to enforce the Fourteenth and Fifteenth Amendments, even though the statutes were buttressed by other constitutional provisions pertaining to voting rights and federal control over elections.

The Screws case involved one of the more cruel episodes in the long and sanguinary history of human brutality. M. Claude Screws, a Georgia sheriff, aided by a special deputy and a policeman, arrested Robert Hall, a Negro, for the theft of a tire, handcuffed him, took him to the courthouse, and beat him to death with a blackjack about eight inches long and weighing two pounds. Screws and his associates were convicted of charges of violating Section 20 of the Criminal Code. In a decision featuring multiple opinions, the Supreme Court reversed the conviction because of defects in the charge to the jury as to intent. Justice Douglas, joined by Justices Black and Reed, gave Section 20 a narrower construction than that applied in the Classic case, in order to avoid constitutional doubts arising out of the vagueness of the general concept of constitutional rights as distinguished from the specific nature of voting rights. Even so, Justice Douglas made it clear that willful violation of Section 20 includes action with a bad purpose in defiance of Court decisions interpreting the Constitution and with reckless disregard of constitutional requirements which have been made specific and definite. Such an interpretation, Justice Douglas also emphasized, was more in line with the traditional balance between state and national powers than the construction urged by Screws or by the government, an important consideration of this opinion throughout.[40]

Justice Rutledge thought the defense that Screws and his

[40] *Screws v. United States,* 325 U.S. 91, 105, 108–109.

associates had merely committed murder contrary to state law, and hence were untouchable under federal statutes, neither pretty nor valid. He spoke of the Fourteenth Amendment and supplementary legislation as being aimed at abusive state powers, to argue that "vague ideas of dual federalism, of ultra vires doctrines imported from private agency, and of want of finality in official action, do not nullify what four years of civil strife secured and eighty years have verified." [41] Accordingly, he was opposed to the strict construction of the statute in the Douglas opinion and in favor of affirming the conviction, but in order to dispose of the case he joined in concurring in the result to break a tie vote caused by the absence of the Chief Justice. Justice Murphy preferred stalemate to injustice, and would have affirmed the conviction. In an opinion permeated with conceptions of dual federalism, Justice Roberts, joined by Justices Frankfurter and Jackson, emphasized a technical conception of state action, to contend that Screws had not acted under color of law, but in violation of it, and hence was only guilty of murder under Georgia law, and that the statutes were unconstitutionally vague.

The decision in the Screws case is naturally weakened by the close division of the Court, but even so it is an important event in constitutional history. It was the first case in which the federal government prosecuted a state official for violating personal rights under the Constitution. The ruling that a state official, even while violating state law, is acting for the state is not new. But as Justice Roberts contended, it is an important concession to congressional power.[42]

In a number of cases dealing with segregation on public conveyances in interstate commerce, the Court has condemned racial discrimination by common carriers acting either voluntarily or in compliance with state segregation laws. Voluntary action by railroads in failing to provide sleeping and adequate dining car service for Negroes under

[41] *Ibid.*, 116.   [42] See also *Baldwin* v. *Franks,* 120 U.S. 678 (1887).

segregation policies was held to violate that section of the Interstate Commerce Act which prohibits all discriminations against persons, and was construed to require equality of treatment for all persons traveling under like circumstances.[43] State legislation applicable to interstate passengers on public conveyances has also been invalidated as an unconstitutional interference with interstate commerce.[44] None of these decisions turned on due process or equal protection, but they are significant as revealing a rigorous judicial attitude toward segregation as a form of discrimination, and as invoking the commerce clause and its vast magnitude of power as a federal weapon against racial discrimination. To the extent that the Interstate Commerce Act was applied to interstate passengers, the decision of the Civil Rights Cases with respect to segregation on public conveyances was vitiated.

Within the climate of judicial opinion prevalent after 1935, it is obvious that racial segregation enforced by state law was in a precarious condition. Hence, when the Supreme Court began the process of burying Jim Crow, judicially but not factually, no student of the Court was surprised. Indeed, in retrospect it is perhaps surprising that the Court took sixteen years to condemn segregation by law.

---

[43] *Mitchell* v. *United States*, 313 U.S. 80 (1941); *Henderson* v. *United States*, 339 U.S. 816 (1950).

[44] *Morgan* v. *Virginia*, 328 U.S. 373 (1946). See, however, *Bob-Lo Excursion Co.* v. *Michigan*, 333 U.S. 28 (1948), in which the Court sustained a state statute prohibiting racial segregation by common carriers as applied to an excursion boat operating between the United States and Canada. The two cases clearly indicate that segregation, not commerce, was the immediate concern of the Court.

CHAPTER SIX

The Judicial Burial
of Jim Crow

THE MOST IMPORTANT DEVELOP-
ment in the Supreme Court's application of constitutional
equality and also one of the major domestic events in the
twentieth century was the Court's condemnation of racial
segregation and its reversal of the separate but equal formula.
Like most constitutional changes, this development did not,
in the manner of Minerva, spring full grown from some
parent judicial brow. The demise of the separate but equal
fiction began in *Missouri* ex rel. *Gaines* v. *Canada*,[1] in a
decision which for the first time extended the Plessy rule
to sustain segregated public school education where the issue
was squarely before the Court. It was also the first case dealing with segregation of the races in public institutions for
higher learning and the first case in which segregation as
applied was held unconstitutional, so that it presents the
paradox that the equal but separate formula underwent
contraction in the very process of expansion. The case was

[1] 305 U.S. 337 (1938). The discussion of educational segregation is based,
with few changes, almost verbatim on my article, "The Constitution,
Education, and Segregation," *loc. cit.*, 415–33.

130

also the first in which the constitutional issues arising out of segregation were adequately argued.

Because Missouri maintained no separate facilities for Negroes in the professional and graduate schools, the state statutes provided for the payment of reasonable tuition fees for attendance at such schools in the universities of adjacent states. When Lloyd Gaines applied for admission to the law school of the University of Missouri he was denied admission solely because it was said to be "contrary to the constitution, laws and public policy of the State to admit a negro as a student in the University of Missouri." [2] Gaines was then told to apply for tuition fees for attendance at a law school in one of the adjoining states which did not segregate Negroes.

After holding the action of the curators of the University of Missouri to be state action within the meaning of the Fourteenth Amendment, Chief Justice Charles Evans Hughes proceeded to apply the "equal but separate" formula. He thereby completed the cycle which began with a formula in a Mississippi transportation statute [3]—a formula that received tacit approval and was extended to education by dictum in the Plessy case [4] and became a rule of law by default in the Gong Lum case.[5] This fact in itself does not make the Gaines case unusual—it is not infrequent in the judicial process for a dictum employing an analogy to be elevated into a rule of law by default of argument. What makes the Gaines case unusual is that the Court looked beyond the formula to question the fiction, and, in law, to question a fiction is to kill it. The constitutionality of laws separating the races in the enjoyment of privileges was held to depend on the quality of those privileges given to the separated groups. In the facts at hand the question then be-

[2] *Ibid.*, 343.
[3] *Louisville, N. O. & T. R. Co.* v. *Mississippi*, 133 U.S. 587 (1890).
[4] *Plessy* v. *Ferguson*, 163 U.S. 537 (1896).
[5] *Gong Lum* v. *Rice*, 275 U.S. 78 (1927).

came one not of the duty of a state to provide legal education or of the quality of education provided, "but of its duty when it provides such training to furnish it to the residents of the State upon the basis of an equality of right." [6]

Accordingly, to provide legal training within the state for whites, while denying it to Negroes and requiring them to go outside the state for legal education, was held a denial of equal rights to the enjoyment of a privilege which the state had created, and the payment of tuition fees for study in another state did not remove the discrimination. Chief Justice Hughes went on to emphasize that "manifestly, the obligation of the State to give the protection of equal laws can be performed only where its laws operate, that is, within its own jurisdiction. It is there that the equality of legal right must be maintained." That there was little demand for the legal education of Negroes was regarded as immaterial, because the right to equal protection does not depend on the number of persons affected. On the contrary, "the essence of the constitutional right is that it is a personal one. . . ." [7] And the fact that the discrimination might be temporary was held to be unimportant because of its possible indefinite continuance, depending on the exercise of a broad discretion by the curators of Lincoln University to organize a law school.

The principles that separate facilities must be in fact equal, and that a state cannot attain the salvation of white supremacy through vicarious atonement by other states for the payment of a fee, were expounded with adequate emphasis to herald future events, even though the Court faltered for a time in 1948 in the Sipuel and Hurst cases by permitting Oklahoma to delay the enforcement of an order directing the admission of a qualified Negro applicant to the University of Oklahoma Law School.[8] However, the Court resumed its march toward constitutional equality in pro-

[6] *Missouri* ex rel. *Gaines* v. *Canada*, 345.   [7] *Ibid.*, 350, 351.
[8] *Sipuel* v. *Board of Regents*, 332 U.S. 631 (1948); *Fisher* v. *Hurst*, 333 U.S. 147 (1948).

fessional and graduate education two years later in *Sweatt* v. *Painter* and *McLaurin* v. *Oklahoma State Regents,* in which segregation in professional and graduate schools was almost totally condemned.[9] These cases were elaborately argued both in the trial courts and the Supreme Court. An impressive record was compiled in the district courts. The records and arguments of the two cases included far more than an exegesis of earlier judicial precedents. Educational statistics, sociological data, and historical research were all mobilized for the elucidation of the issues presented.

After the Gaines and Sipuel decisions Texas, along with other southern states, had provided separate facilities for professional education in the hope of maintaining the "equal but separate" fiction. In *Sweatt* v. *Painter* strenuous but unsuccessful efforts were made by respondents to demonstrate the equality between the newly established Negro law school and the law school maintained at the University of Texas for whites. The spectacular differences between the two schools were so obvious that even the most obtuse could not overlook them. Equally important, inequalities of segregated education were presented for the record with consummate adroitness by Mr. Thurgood Marshall of the NAACP. The record disclosed, for example, that segregation in education was then sanctioned and enforced by law in seventeen states.[10] In 1949 there were two accredited medical schools for Negroes in the South and twenty-nine for whites, two accredited schools of pharmacy for Negroes and twenty for whites, two accredited law schools for Negroes (one provisionally) and forty for whites, no engineering schools for Negroes and thirty-six for whites.[11]

[9] 339 U.S. 629 (1950); 339 U.S. 637 (1950), respectively.
[10] Alabama, Arkansas, Delaware, Florida, Georgia, Kentucky, Louisiana, Maryland, Mississippi, Missouri, North Carolina, Oklahoma, South Carolina, Tennessee, Texas, Virginia, and West Virginia. In addition to these states, segregated education was permissive or mandatory at different levels in Arizona, Kansas, and New Mexico. See Konvitz, *The Constitution and Civil Rights,* 132–34.
[11] Brief for Petitioner, appendix, ix, *Sweatt* v. *Painter,* 631.

The brief for Sweatt cited data to demonstrate further that physical equality is not possible under a system of enforced segregation. Thus in 1949 Negroes constituted 7.7 per cent of the population of the United States and southern whites, 26.7 per cent. The South was then spending 22.3 per cent of the national total for higher education. Of this percentage Negroes received 1.8 per cent and whites received 20.5 per cent, or a per capita expenditure of $4.28 for whites and $1.32 for Negroes. Sixteen per cent of the white universities were accredited by the American Association of Universities, only 5.1 per cent of Negro institutions were so accredited, and except for Howard University, which is federally financed, there was no publicly supported accredited Negro institution of higher learning. Such variations in expenditure were inevitably reflected in qualitative and quantitative differences in curricula, faculties, libraries, laboratories, and general physical facilities.[12]

Chief Justice Vinson, for a unanimous court, in the Sweatt case repeated the familiar rule that the Court will not decide constitutional issues outside the context of a particular case, and even then will draw such decisions as narrowly as possible.[13] Hence he declared, "much of the excellent research and detailed argument presented in these cases is unnecessary to their disposition." [14] The Court accordingly refused to re-examine *Plessy* v. *Ferguson* and thereby passively approved the "equal but separate" fiction. However, it proceeded to look beyond the fiction in such a penetrating manner as to render it meaningless and inapplicable. On the basis of the record and the briefs, the contents of which were perhaps more influential than the Chief Justice indicated, the Court then noted the sharp disparities between the two law schools with respect to the size and quality of their faculties,

---

[12] *Ibid.*, 63–64.
[13] *Ibid.*, 631, citing *Rescue Army* v. *Municipal Court*, 331 U.S. 549 (1947).
[14] *Sweatt* v. *Painter*, 631.

the size of their respective student bodies and libraries, the presence of a chapter of the Order of the Coif at the white law school (which its dean testified was insignificant in terms of instructional equality) and the absence of a chapter at the law school for Negroes, the existence of a law review at the University of Texas and the lack of one at the Negro school, the accredited status of the white law school and the lack of such status of the other, and the positions of distinction and power occupied by the alumni of the University of Texas in the legal profession and public life of the state and nation in startling contrast to the solitary and almost anonymous alumnus of the Negro law school who had become a member of the Texas bar. As though this were not enough to dispose of the issue of equality between the two institutions, the Court went on to say: "What is more important, the University of Texas Law School possesses to a far greater degree those qualities which are incapable of objective measurement but which make for greatness in a law school. Such qualities . . . include reputation of the faculty, experience of the administration, position and influence of the alumni, standing in the community, traditions and prestige. It is difficult to believe that one who had a free choice between these law schools would consider the question close." [15]

The Court also referred to the law as a highly learned profession and to the law school as a proving ground for legal learning and practice which is not and cannot be effective "in isolation from individuals and institutions with which the law interacts." By excluding from the Negro law school 85 per cent of the population of Texas, including most of the lawyers, witnesses, jurors, judges, and other officials with whom Sweatt would be dealing as an attorney, the state was in another way denying the substantial equality guaranteed by the Fourteenth Amendment. The argument that reciprocal exclusion of whites and Negroes from the

[15] *Ibid.*, 634.

respective schools produced no inequality was regarded as inconsistent with realities. "Equal protection of the laws is not achieved through indiscriminate imposition of inequalities." [16]

What all this means in effect is that separate educational facilities can never be equal. Quantitative equality in terms of the size of the faculty, student body, floor space in buildings, volumes in the library, and the like is possible. Qualitative equality in terms of the reputation and prestige of faculty and alumni, opportunities for contacts with future jurists, recognition by the Order of the Coif, and other factors which make for the greatness of an institution is not susceptible of measurement, even by the initiated, and such equality is not immediately attainable by any newly established professional school regardless of how lavishly it is financed or how vigorously it is promoted. In professional and graduate schools, at least, *Sweatt* v. *Painter* in its practical application required identical facilities. This conclusion is fortified by the ruling in *McLaurin* v. *Oklahoma State Regents*,[17] even though this case can be interpreted narrowly to mean no more than that once a state university admits a student to its graduate or professional schools, it cannot in any way discriminate against him.

The facts of the McLaurin case present an exercise in the accommodation of educational institutions to new rules of law contrary to existing customs, traditions, and usages, thus rather effectively disposing of Justice Brown's homily in the Plessy case on the inefficacy of law as a means of social control in race relations. G. W. McLaurin had been admitted as a graduate student in education by the University of Oklahoma upon the order of a statutory three-judge district court. Once admitted, however, he was subjected to varying degrees of discrimination made mandatory by amendments to

---

[16] *Ibid.*, 634, 635, quoting *Shelley* v. *Kraemer*, 334 U.S. 1, 22 (1948).
[17] 339 U.S. 637 (1950).

the state law providing for the admission of Negroes on a segregated basis under rules and regulations formulated by the president. Immediately after admission McLaurin was required to sit at a designated desk in an anteroom adjoining the main classroom, to sit at a designated table on the mezzanine floor of the library, and to sit at a specified table and eat at different times from other students in the university cafeteria. McLaurin applied to a federal district court for relief from these discriminations, but the court denied his motion for an amended order. McLaurin then appealed to the Supreme Court.

In the time between the decision of the district court and the hearing before the Supreme Court, the University of Oklahoma modified its policy of intramural segregation. McLaurin was permitted to move into the main classroom, but was required at first to sit in an area surrounded by a rail bearing the sign "Reserved For Colored." Later he was moved to a seat in a row specified for Negroes. He was permitted to go to the main floor of the library, but was assigned a specific table. He was also permitted to eat in the cafeteria at the same time as other students, but at a reserved table. The university contended that these restrictions were merely nominal, but McLaurin maintained successfully that the restrictions denied him the substantial equality of right guaranteed by the Fourteenth Amendment.

Again the Supreme Court refused to rule that segregation in itself is illegal or to re-examine the Plessy rule. In his opinion for a unanimous Court, Chief Justice Vinson pointed to the effects that McLaurin's education would have on those he would teach in the future. Thus the education and development of his students would suffer "to the extent that his training is unequal to that of his classmates." That McLaurin might still be set apart by his fellow students after the removal of the restrictions was regarded as irrelevant, for "there is a vast difference—a Constitutional difference—between restrictions imposed by the state which prohibit the intellectual commingling of students, and the refusal of individuals to commingle where the state presents no such bar." [18] Accordingly the Court concluded that the restrictions imposed on McLaurin set him apart from other students, handicapped his graduate study, and impaired and inhibited his ability to engage in discussion and exchange views with other students and in general to learn his profession.

Even though the Court refused to repudiate the "equal but separate" rule, the Sweatt and McLaurin cases effectively pronounced a constitutional doom on segregated public education. The test of the validity of segregation laws in these cases continued to be the test of reasonableness, but in determining the reasonableness of segregation laws the Court no longer, as in *Plessy* v. *Ferguson,* looked to the customs and traditions of the people, but to the actual equality of the separate facilities and to the principle as stated in the McLaurin case that segregation and discrimination in the use of identical facilities cannot be imposed for their own sake. Once the Court emphasized equal facilities to the point of requiring identical facilities on a nondiscriminatory basis, there could no longer be a constitutional justification for segregated education, whatever differences might be found between higher education and elementary or intermediate education. However, by refusing to reject the "equal but separate" formula the Court retained a measure of discretion in the adjudication of future segregation cases either by looking at the physical facts and finding existing inequalities, or by ultimately reversing the Plessy rule, as it did in the Public School Segregation Cases.[19]

[18] *Ibid.,* 641.
[19] 347 U.S. 483 (1954). Four cases arising in Delaware, Kansas, Virginia, and South Carolina were consolidated for the disposition of the proceedings. All except that in Delaware came to the Supreme Court on appeals from federal district courts. The Delaware case came up on certiorari from the state supreme court.

It had, of course, been a matter of common knowledge long before the Public School Segregation Cases that state authorities never troubled themselves to apply the formula of separate and equal other than to keep the races separate in public places, with the result that segregation in practice imposed a progressive series of discriminations on Negroes as a class. But the formula had never been documented officially so thoroughly until the segregation cases. If a Negro travelled by rail he was assigned to a dingy car near the locomotive and denied access to dining and sleeping cars. If he found himself away from home, or if he still does, he was and is denied on grounds of race access to adequate hotels or restaurants and sometimes access to any accommodations. If a Negro child went to school he was housed in a poor building, perhaps far away from the white schools past which he walked or rode in a dilapidated bus so worn out by transporting white children that it was regarded as all right for Negroes. He was, in turn, denied the curricula afforded white children and, perhaps fortunately for his education, the more expensive gadgets and techniques (so abundantly devised for public education by teachers' colleges) for imparting learning without study and advancing such anti-intellectual objectives as adjusted living and democratic conformity. With a poor education at best, and being black, he found most of the professions and many of the common callings closed to him. Finally, when he became a parent and sent his children to school, it was to a school in which he or his race had little and most often no voice with respect to administration, choice of curricula, and so on.

The decisions in the Gaines, Sweatt, and McLaurin cases stimulated frenzied spending campaigns and gigantic efforts in the states with segregated education in order to equalize the educational opportunities of white and Negro pupils. Effective as these efforts were in producing blueprints of gaudy new Negro schools for the brave new world, they came too late to deter either Negroes in their quest for equality or the Supreme Court in its role as the major organ for the enforcement of equality before the law. Accordingly, at the very time that the first serious measures were being taken to convert the fiction of separate but equal into physical reality, suits were pending which were to seal its doom.

The segregation cases came to the Court on the basis of elaborate records compiled in trials in the lower federal and state courts. As in the Sweatt case, the NAACP prepared its cases with great care and executed a brilliant plan of strategy and tactics in litigation. In all of the cases in the trial courts, counsel for the Negro plaintiffs relied on the testimony of school officials and private citizens, to show great variations between the physical facilities, curricula, and the quality of instruction provided for white children and those afforded to Negroes.

In the cases coming from Clarendon County, South Carolina, and Prince Edward County, Virginia, among the poorer counties in their respective states, the differences were most pronounced. In Clarendon County, South Carolina, for example, there were 2,375 white and 6,631 Negro pupils, but a total of $395,000 was expended for the white schools in contrast to $282,000 for Negro schools, or a per capita expenditure of $166.74 for whites and $43.17 for Negroes. Comparisons of the number of pupils per school, room, and teacher, and physical facilities in terms of drinking fountains, toilet facilities, and auditoriums and gymnasiums revealed significant discrepancies. At the Negro schools there were no drinking fountains, and at two of the three Negro schools there were even no desks. The white schools had indoor flush-toilet facilities, but the Negro schools were provided with outdoor earth toilets. The Negro schools had neither an auditorium nor a gymnasium, whereas the white elementary school had an auditorium and the white high school a gymnasium. A larger number of academic and preskill subjects were taught in the white schools, whereas the curricula at the Negro schools consisted of agriculture, home economics, vocational agriculture, and some academic subjects.[20]

Similar contrasts appeared in Prince Edward County, Virginia, where there were central buildings for whites and central and tar outbuildings for Negroes, with an average of $1,679 per pupil invested in the buildings for whites and $306 in those for Negroes. Cafeteria facilities were provided in one white high school, but none at the Negro and a second white high school. Disparities in equipment and libraries to the disadvantage of the Negro were also revealed. In terms of college degrees the white teachers were better trained; they were also more experienced and better paid. Altogether, fifteen busses were provided for white pupils and nine for Negroes, and the nine were hand-downs from the whites. Although some of the same disparities existed between the two white high schools as between the better high school for whites and the Negro high school, the discrepancies between Negro and white facilities in their totality were obvious. Some of these discrepancies, to be sure, arose from poverty, but even so there was an evident pattern of discrimination against Negroes in the competition for facilities which were inadequate at best in an impoverished rural county.[21] Other discrepancies were due to gifts of books to the better of the white high schools and to the provision for a cafeteria by the Parent-Teachers Association,[22] but most of them were officially and deliberately planned by the county school board.

In addition to stressing the physical and intrinsic inequalities between white and Negro schools, counsel for the NAACP introduced much testimony from social psycholo-

[20] Transcript of Record, 40, 50–56, in *Briggs* v. *Elliott,* 347 U.S. 483.
[21] Transcript of Record, 47, 87, 93–115, in *Davis* v. *County School Board,* 347 U.S. 483.
[22] *Ibid.,* 384, 392, 393.

gists, educationists, and sociologists to the effect that segregated education of itself, independently of the quantity and quality of facilities, is detrimental to those who are segregated by producing harmful effects on their emotional, physical, and financial status.[23] Counsel for South Carolina and Virginia denied these contentions, which they argued were matters of opinion rather than of demonstrable scientific fact, but they introduced testimony to the effect that segregated education was less harmful than mixed schools, apparently unaware of the inconsistency of such testimony with their contentions concerning the unscientific opinions of social psychologists. They adduced evidence to show, too, that the abolition of segregated education would result in the destruction of the public schools, and argued later that in any event the case presented issues of policy to be determined by the legislature and not by the courts.[24]

The segregation cases were thoroughly argued before the Supreme Court during the 1952 term, but the Court approached a final decision warily and ordered reargument on five questions. These dealt, first, with whether the Thirty-ninth Congress, which submitted, and the state legislatures, which ratified, the Fourteenth Amendment contemplated that it would abolish segregation in public schools; second, whether Congress, under the fifth section of the amendment, could abolish such segregation, or whether it would be within the judicial power in the light of future conditions to construe the amendment as abolishing educational segregation of its own force; and, third, should the answers to the second question not dispose of the issue, whether it would be within the judicial power to abolish segregation in the public schools.[25]

---

[23] Transcript of Record in *Briggs* v. *Elliott,* 83–90, 133.
[24] Brief for South Carolina, 19, in *Briggs* v. *Elliott.*
[25] *Brown* v. *Board of Education,* 345 U.S. 972 (1953). On the basis of all previous decisions construing the equal protection and due process clauses of the Fourteenth Amendment, that part of the second question dealing with its effect and the third question were gratuitous, because in all

Two final questions had to do with alternative methods of enforcement in the event the Court should find segregated public school education a denial of equal protection.

On the basis of the decisions in the Sweatt and McLaurin cases and in view of the facts established in the record, despite frantic efforts on the part of Virginia and South Carolina to equalize white and colored education by providing better physical facilities for Negro than for white pupils, the Court had no choice but to declare segregation as applied in the cases at bar a denial of the equal protection of the laws. In so declaring, however, it was confronted with a choice of alternatives. First, it could have continued, as in the Sweatt case, to retain the so-called "equal but separate" principle while carefully scrutinizing the particular facilities under consideration to ascertain whether they were in fact equal. This approach would have had the possible advantage of leaving precedents undisturbed, of accepting the general admissions of Virginia and South Carolina that conditions in white and Negro schools in Clarendon and Prince Edward counties were not substantially equal at the time of the litigation, and of taking the full advantage of the facts of record which revealed the vast differences between white and Negro education.

Such a course, however, was fraught with grave disadvantages. It would have resulted in endless litigation in those innumerable instances in which local school authorities still under superficial color of law could deny equality of education to colored children. It would have been followed inevitably by increased spending by the southern states to equalize their school systems, with the ensuing result that the Court would have continued to be confronted with the alternatives of condoning segregation where facilities were

previous cases the Court acted on the assumption that the amendment condemned all violations of its own force and that the judiciary was the primary organ for its enforcement.

substantially equal, of adopting criteria, as in the Sweatt case, which in effect render the "equal but separate" principle impossible to apply, or of applying the requirements of the McLaurin case, where the facilities were actually identical. Furthermore, disposal of the cases in this manner would have meant continued repudiation of that ideal of political, civil, and legal equality which the American nation as a people never wearies of preaching to or imposing on other peoples.

A second alternative, and by far the more feasible, would have been the reversal of the Plessy case simply on the basis of its conflict with the reasoning of earlier decisions to the effect that the equal protection clause prohibits all state or official action of an unreasonably discriminatory nature. As already noted, such a decision had been rendered in *Strauder* v. *West Virginia*,[26] in which the Court invalidated a state statute which excluded Negroes from service on juries and grand juries on the ground that the Fourteenth Amendment "was designed to assure to the colored race the enjoyment of all the civil rights that under the law are enjoyed by white persons." It may be well to reiterate, too, that the Court with repetitious emphasis asserted that "the law in the States shall be the same for the black as for the white; that all persons, whether colored or white, shall stand equal before the laws of the States and, in regard to the colored race, for whose protection the Amendment was primarily designed, that no discrimination shall be made against them by law because of their color."

If the amendment, as the Court said, guaranteed Negroes a "positive immunity," or "the right" to exemption "from unfriendly legislation against them distinctively as colored," and "from legal discriminations, implying inferiority in civil society, lessening the security of their enjoyment of the rights which others enjoy, and discriminations which are steps towards reducing them to the condition of a subject race," [27]

[26] 100 U.S. 303 (1880). See Chapter 4.   [27] *Ibid.*, 306, 307.

then the Strauder case alone was ample precedent for the reversal of the Plessy case. However, the Strauder decision is reinforced by those in *Virginia* v. *Rives* and *Ex parte Virginia*.[28] Even Justice Bradley's restrictive opinion in the Civil Rights Cases,[29] in which the Court, out of hypersensitivity to the maintenance of federalism as it existed prior to the Civil War and the postwar amendments, narrowly construed the power of Congress to enforce the amendment, is clear on the issue that all state-imposed discrimination is a denial of equal protection. Instead of making full use of these precedents, the Chief Justice made the least use of them. He quoted from the Strauder case and cited the others, but only in a footnote to his narration of the history of the "equal but separate" doctrine.[30] The Court could have stressed also the results of the administration of educational segregation and could have brought segregation within the Yick Wo[31] rule that even though a statute be valid on its face it will fall if administered with such an evil eye and unequal hand as to bring it within the substance of the prohibition of the equal protection clause. Finally, the Court could have found the Plessy rule inconsistent with the combined results of the Sweatt and McLaurin cases.

A third possible, but hardly feasible, ground for reversing the "equal but separate" rule might have been found in the historical origins of the Fourteenth Amendment, the circumstances leading to its adoption and ratification, and the "intentions" of its framers. A wealth of pertinent historical materials had been laboriously presented in briefs and appendices by counsel on reargument. Such a course would have presented a number of obstacles, not the least of which would have been to distinguish between the subjective motivations of the individual members of Congress and the

[28] 100 U.S. 313 (1880); 100 U.S. 339 (1880).   [29] 109 U.S. 3 (1883).
[30] *Brown* v. *Board of Education*, 347 U.S. 483, 490, note 5.
[31] *Yick Wo* v. *Hopkins*, 118 U.S. 356 (1886).

ratifying legislatures and the objective intent of a legislative assembly as a corporate body. For the most part, the debates on the Fourteenth Amendment and on kindred subjects, like the Civil Rights and Freedmen's Bureau bills of 1866, as discussed by counsel, were revealing with respect to some of the subjective intentions of the active framers (who constituted a minority of the membership of the Thirty-ninth Congress), but hardly adequate as answers to the precise questions posed by the Court.

A second obstacle to having recourse to the intention of the framers is the number and variety of motives back of the adoption of the Fourteenth Amendment. One intention which the Radicals certainly had, as revealed on the face of the second and third sections, was to make the South and the country safe for the Republican party by disfranchising the bulk of the southern whites because of their participation in rebellion and by indirectly enfranchising the Negroes, and then establishing governments under the joint control of Negroes, "carpetbaggers," and "scalawags." [32] Intermingled with the realistic and sordid motives underlying these two sections were the noble and idealistic sentiments and aspirations of human equality, individual liberty, and the essential dignity of all men regardless of race or color. These aspirations found expression in the first section dealing with the privileges and immunities of citizenship, due process of law, and the equal protection of the laws. Finally, there were undoubtedly some who neither understood nor cared about what they were

---

[32] At various stages in the debate on the proposed Fourteenth Amendment, political considerations emerged as exemplified in the speeches of Stevens, who frequently raised the specter of a Congress dominated by traitors and Democrats, between whom little or no distinction was made. Typical of these utterances are the questions of Representative William D. ("Pig Iron") Kelley: "Who ought to govern this country? The men who for more than four years sustained bloody war for its overthrow, or they whom my colleague [Boyer] designates as that proscriptive body of men known as the great Union party who sustained the government against the most gigantic rebellion since that which Satan led?" *Cong. Globe,* 39th Cong., 1st Sess., 2448. For Stevens' fears see *ibid.,* 2544.

doing so long as they did not run afoul of the Radical leadership or risk political defeat in their home constituencies. All of these factors constitute the most serious hazards in coming to any final conclusion with respect to the understanding of the Thirty-ninth Congress concerning the application of the Fourteenth Amendment specifically to segregated education, a subject which was mentioned but hardly discussed.

Because of the confusions and contradictions in the evidence pertaining to the understanding of the Congress which submitted the Fourteenth Amendment and of the state legislatures which ratified it, it is small wonder that Chief Justice Warren, in his opinion in the Public School Segregation Cases, found the evidence concerning the intentions of the framers of the Fourteenth Amendment inconclusive at best. Instead, therefore, of relying upon history, which in these cases would have been a slender reed unless the Court had invented a historical fiction, as it has done occasionally,[33] and instead of invoking earlier precedents which could have provided strong support, the Chief Justice based his opinion on the quicksands of social psychology, reinforced by vastly changed conditions in education between 1868, when the Fourteenth Amendment was adopted, and 1954, when these cases were decided.

In approaching the problem of the validity of segregated education, according to the Chief Justice, the Court could not turn the clock back to 1868, when the Fourteenth Amendment was adopted, and to 1896, when the Plessy case was decided. Rather, it had to consider public school education "in the light of its full development and its present place in

---

[33] Marshall's conception of the Constitution as emanating from all the people is such a fiction, and Justice Black's dissenting conclusion in *Adamson* v. *California*, 332 U.S. 46, 70–74 (1947), may belong in this category. From the standpoint of things that were not so at all, historical fictions were employed in *Pollock* v. *Farmers' Loan & Trust Co.*, 157 U.S. 429, 158 U.S. 601 (1895), by Chief Justice Melville Fuller concerning the meaning of the term "direct tax."

American life throughout the Nation." [34] He went on to indicate that today "education is perhaps the most important function of state and local governments. . . . It is required in the performance of our most basic public responsibilities, even service in the armed forces. It is the very foundation of good citizenship. Today it is a principal instrument in awakening the child to cultural values, in preparing him for later professional training, and in helping him to adjust normally to his environment." [35] The Chief Justice quoted with approval the finding of the federal district court in the Kansas case to the effect that segregation in the public schools has a detrimental effect on colored children by denoting inferiority and thereby affecting the motivation of the child to learn and retarding the educational and mental development he would receive in a racially integrated school. He went on to say that "whatever may have been the extent of psychological knowledge at the time of *Plessy* v. *Ferguson,* this finding is amply supported by modern authority." Any language in *Plessy* v. *Ferguson* to the contrary was accordingly rejected, and the Court concluded that "in the field of public education the doctrine of 'separate but equal' has no place. Separate educational facilities are inherently unequal." [36]

Seldom, if ever, has the Supreme Court of the United States reversed an earlier decision without finding either (1) that the case was erroneously decided at the time of decision on the basis of conflict with history or of inconsistency with then existing precedent, or (2) that the case has not been followed subsequently and is indeed in conflict with later decisions. The Court has never been more candid in basing a reversal of precedent on changing conditions and new developments alone than it was here. The Court at no place said that *Plessy* v. *Ferguson* was erroneously decided in 1896. Indeed, the

[34] *Brown* v. *Board of Education,* 492–93. [35] *Ibid.,* 493.
[36] *Ibid.,* 494–95.

implication is that *Plessy* v. *Ferguson* had become bad because of the growth of public education from the crude and precarious thing it was in 1868 and 1896 into the all-encompassing and grandiose thing it had become by 1954, and because of advances in psychological knowledge.

By now, of course, it is no longer a novelty for the Court to reverse its earlier decisions or even to advance the concept of adapting the law to meet changes in social conditions, but it is a rarity to the point of novelty for the Court to do either completely outside the framework of history or of litigated cases decided either previously or subsequently. And, as noted above, it was unnecessary for the Court to do so here. All it had to do was to hold that the "equal but separate" formula, when applied by a state or its officials, was not in accord with precedents before and after 1896, and that accordingly *Plessy* v. *Ferguson* was reversed. Such a course would have combined both the concept of constitutional growth through judicial interpretation and an adherence to precedent in the orderly development of the organic law, and it would have rendered the Court less vulnerable to criticism to the effect that the decision was sheer judicial legislation.

By all criteria, however, the *decision* in the segregation cases was a great decision. The *opinion,* on the other hand, was not. Indeed, after the elaborate arguments adduced in briefs and supplements of counsel, the opinion was something of an anticlimax and did not reach "the height of this great argument" to assert equality before the law and to justify the ways of the law to man. Moreover, the Court's opinion lacked the vigor and conviction of the dissents of the earlier Justice Harlan in other cases dealing with segregation,[37] and it fell short of the legal craftsmanship of more recent opinions by Chief Justice Hughes,[38] Justice Cardozo,[39] and Justice

---

[37] *Berea College* v. *Kentucky*, 211 U.S. 45, 58 (1908); Civil Rights Cases, 109 U.S. 3 (1883).
[38] *West Coast Hotel Co.* v. *Parrish*, 300 U.S. 379 (1937).
[39] *Steward Machine Co.* v. *Davis*, 301 U.S. 548 (1937).

Stone,[40] which changed the course of the law by reversing
earlier decisions. However, despite its deficiencies in rhetoric
and craftsmanship, the opinion is still in the great tradition
of constitutional growth by judicial interpretation initiated
by Chief Justice Marshall and continued by such illustrious
successors as Justice Holmes, whose words are as applicable
to the Fourteenth Amendment as to the Constitution it
changed. Justice Holmes said: "When we are dealing with
words that also are a constituent act, like the Constitution
of the United States, we must realize that they have called
into life a being, the development of which could not have
been foreseen completely by the most gifted of its begetters.
. . . The case before us must be considered in the light of
our whole experience, and not merely in that of what was
said a hundred years ago." [41]

This is what Chief Justice Warren must have had in mind
in his references to the great changes in public education and
his assertion that we cannot turn the clock back to 1868 or
even to 1896. Much has happened to the Negro, to education,
and to the Constitution which could not have been foreseen
by Thaddeus Stevens or Jacob Howard. Not the least of what
has occurred was the atrophy of the fifth section of the Fourteenth Amendment as a result both of judicial decisions and
of the continuing influence of Calhoun, whose mischievous
device of the concurrent veto finds current expression in the
Senate filibuster and the seniority rule in the organization of
congressional committees, either of which is a sufficient bar-
rier to legislative implementation of the Fourteenth Amendment. If the Fourteenth Amendment is to have meaning, the
Court must provide it, and in doing so it must have regard
to all relevant factors. The decision of the Court in the segregation cases, by looking upon the Constitution as a process
of growth, and by bringing constitutional interpretation

[40] *United States* v. *Darby*, 312 U.S. 100 (1941).
[41] *Missouri* v. *Holland*, 252 U.S. 416, 433 (1920).

nearer to the American ideal of the equality of all men in the enjoyment of legal privileges and immunities, is bound to occupy a prominent place in constitutional history long after analysts have ceased to write about it and the strident voices of neonullificationists have been stilled.

A final phase of the Public School Segregation Cases of some importance is the assimilation of equal protection into due process of law in *Bolling* v. *Sharpe*,[42] in which the Court invalidated segregation in the public schools of the District of Columbia as a violation of the due process clause of the Fifth Amendment, and thereby returned to the merger of due process and equal protection so common in the congressional debate on the Fourteenth Amendment. Although the equal protection clause does not limit federal power, congressional legislation was frequently challenged between 1911 and 1954 as making arbitrary discriminations in violation of due process of law,[43] and the Court just as frequently sustained the legislation. However, in so doing it usually decided the issue as raised upon its merits and thereby tacitly assumed that due process forbids invidious and arbitrary discriminations.[44] The decision in *Bolling* v. *Sharpe* not only held expressly that due process of law condemns federal discriminations based on race or color, but it was the first decision to invalidate congressional policy on this basis. Distinctions based on race "must be scrutinized with particular

---

[42] 347 U.S. 497 (1954).   [43] *Flint* v. *Stone Tracy Co.*, 220 U.S. 107 (1911).
[44] *Billings* v. *United States*, 232 U.S. 261 (1914); *Barclay* v. *Edwards*, 267 U.S. 442 (1924); *Hill* v. *United States* ex rel. *Weiner*, 300 U.S. 105 (1937); *Steward Machine Co.* v. *Davis*, 301 U.S. 548 (1937); *Carmichael* v. *Southern Coal and Coke Co.*, 301 U.S. 495 (1937); *Currin* v. *Wallace*, 306 U.S. 1 (1939); *United States* v. *Rock Royal Cooperative*, 307 U.S. 533, 563–68 (1939). Of these, the Carmichael and Rock Royal cases are of special significance. Also especially significant are those based on race or ancestry, *Hiyabayashi* v. *United States*, 320 U.S. 81, 100 (1943); *Korematsu* v. *United States*, 323 U.S. 214 (1944), which the Court has said "by their very nature are odious to a free people whose institutions are founded upon the doctrine of equality." See also *Detroit Bank* v. *United States*, 317 U.S. 329, 337, 338 (1943).

care," said Chief Justice Warren, "because they are contrary to our traditions and hence constitutionally suspect." [45] Liberty, the Chief Justice indicated, cannot be restricted except for a proper governmental objective. Segregation in public education is not related to any proper governmental objective, and thereby "imposes on Negro children of the District of Columbia a burden that constitutes an arbitrary deprivation of their liberty" contrary to the due process clause of the Fifth Amendment.[46]

By extending the rule of the segregation cases both to other public facilities and to segregation imposed by private systems, and by its broader conception of state action in the suffrage cases, the Court has done more than seriously shake the rule in the Civil Rights Cases and overturn *Plessy* v. *Ferguson*. Indeed, since 1935 it has worked a constitutional revolution, as distinguished from much actual social change, in the federal law of race relations. And, remarkable as this is, it is perhaps just as amazing that it has done so with a minimum of disturbance of earlier precedents. Contrary to those critics of the Court whose purpose is to inflame rather than to inform, only two previous decisions have been overruled. One of these was *Grovey* v. *Townsend*,[47] decided in 1935 and reversed in 1944 in the Allwright case,[48] which had hardly become hallowed by the sanctity associated with age. The other, *Plessy* v. *Ferguson*, was contrary to an impressive group of decisions which preceded and followed it, inconsistent with the social facts of segregated education, and had not been followed in the Sweatt and McLaurin cases in 1950. From the standpoint of all the precedents and from the history and text of the Fourteenth and Fifteenth amendments, *Smith* v. *Allwright* and *Brown* v. *Topeka Board of Education* are much better law than the decisions they reversed.

[45] *Bolling* v. *Sharpe*, 499, citing *Gibson* v. *Mississippi*, 162 U.S. 565 (1896).
[46] *Bolling* v. *Sharpe*, 499–500.   [47] 295 U.S. 45.
[48] *Smith* v. *Allwright*, 321 U.S. 649.

Another important aspect of the Court's work in the area of equal rights is the continuing concern which the Court has shown for the maintenance of the federal system. Respect for the power of the states to control their internal affairs is a persistent theme of the opinions in the Screws case [49] and the jury cases and is implicit in the Court's later refusal to invalidate Alabama's pupil placement law as an unconstitutional denial of equal protection on its face.[50] The picture which some critics, out of ignorance or malice, have sought to draw of the Court as a ruthless destroyer of states' rights is just as much out of accord with reality as the idea of a Court that is reckless with precedent to the point of usurping the power to amend the Constitution. Whatever may be said in criticism of the Court's decisions involving equal rights must be tempered by an acknowledgment that these decisions are backed by impressive precedents, are warranted by the text of the Constitution, and are an expression of the revolutionary ideals of the American Republic as borrowed from the Stoic philosophers, the Christian Fathers, and John Locke, and as given vitality by Jefferson and other American Revolutionaries. Altogether, therefore, the Court has done no more than reaffirm the traditional American doctrine of equality before the law and revitalize in part the power of Congress to implement it if the states fail in their responsibilities. This falls far short of establishing equality in all aspects of human relations, desecrating the ark of the covenant, or usurping legislation or state powers.

Just as the Supreme Court's decisions in the suffrage cases have not eliminated discrimination because of race or color in voting, the rulings in the Public School Segregation Cases and cases following it [51] have not eliminated segregation en-

---

[49] *Screws* v. *United States,* 325 U.S. 91 (1945)

[50] *Shuttlesworth* v. *Birmingham Board of Education,* 358 U.S. 101 (1958).

[51] As a result of the decision in *Brown* v. *Board of Education,* the federal courts have condemned segregation by law in publicly supported parks and recreation facilities, publicly operated restaurants, public transportation

forced by public authority. Segregation by law soon disappeared in the District of Columbia, where the public schools were quickly adjusted to racial integration. Somewhat more slowly, but in good faith, the border states of Delaware, Kentucky, Maryland, Missouri, Oklahoma, and West Virginia began to process the desegregation. Token integration occurred in Arkansas, North Carolina, Tennessee, Virginia, and portions of Texas, where some areas followed the patterns of the border and others that of the Deep South, where no integration had taken place by 1959.

Altogether, 734 of 2,881 biracial school districts in the southern region had been desegregated five years after the Court's decision, but 590 of these were in the District of Columbia and the border, 125 in Texas, and 19 in the upper South. With respect to the number of pupils affected, the picture was much the same, with 447,022 Negro pupils of a total of almost 3,000,000 placed in integrated situations, as distinguished from less than 300,000 actually enrolled in mixed schools. Here, too, the preponderance of Negroes affected was in the District of Columbia and the border, with only 206 Negroes enrolled in previously all-white schools in North Carolina, Arkansas, Tennessee, and Virginia.[52]

Many of the states in the South, in addition to noncompliance with the Court's decision, pursued policies of aggressive defiance. Official resistance took such forms as public school closing and leasing laws, pupil placement laws, interposition resolutions, closing of schools by executive proclamation, and executive maintenance of segregated education by force in the name of law and order, as exemplified by the employment of state police by Governor Allan Shivers to maintain

facilities, and the like. For these cases see individual issues of the *Race Relations Law Reporter* published by the Vanderbilt University School of Law.

[52] Southern Education Reporting Service, *Status of School Segregation-Desegregation in the Southern and Border States* (Nashville, 1959). Most helpful also is the *Southern School News* published by the same group.

segregated education in Mansfield, Texas, and employment of the National Guard by Governor Orval Faubus in Little Rock to prevent nine children from entering Central High School. Semiofficial and unofficial defiance has also been common in the states of the former Confederacy. Leaders of thought and opinion in politics and journalism employed the ancient shibboleth, "a government of laws and not of men," to encourage lawlessness under labels like "massive resistance," as proposed by Senator Harry Byrd, and resistance by all legal means, as advocated by one hundred southern congressmen who signed the so-called Southern Manifesto. Most of the politicians and editors who urged resistance did not overtly advocate violence, but their intemperate language and distortion of the law created an atmosphere conducive to disorder generally and encouraged such sporadic outbreaks of violence which resulted in mob action at Little Rock, Mansfield, and Clinton, Tennessee, and in bombings of schools, synagogues, or churches in Nashville, Clinton, Atlanta, Birmingham, and Jacksonville.[53]

Except for President Eisenhower's use of troops to prevent obstruction, by official and mob lawlessness, to the enforcement of a federal court order in Little Rock, federal response to southern resistance was hardly noticeable. In some instances the Department of Justice intervened in local suits in federal courts to argue as *amicus curiae* for the implementation of the decision of 1954. Congress responded only indirectly with the Civil Rights Acts of 1957 and 1960, mild statutes reinforcing the right to vote and providing for general investigations of denials of equal protection of the laws. Other-

[53] For a detailed account of official measures of resistance see "Race Relations Law Survey, May, 1954–May, 1957" in 2 *Race Relations Law Reporter*, 881 (1957); and Don Shoemaker, "With All Deliberate Speed," 137 *New Republic*, 9 (1957). Individual issues of the *Race Relations Law Reporter* contain the texts of federal and state court decisions, acts of Congress and state legislatures, administrative orders, and executive pronouncements in the whole area of race relations. This publication is indispensable to a student of the law of race relations.

wise the President confined his role in the segregation crisis to pronouncements at his press conferences, hardly an adequate or effective forum for the enunciation of public policies. Although there was little that the President could legally do in the crisis prior to Governor Shivers' defiance in 1956 and that of Governor Faubus in 1957, it is possible that he could have mitigated the effects of the crisis through vigorous moral and political leadership and the employment of his personal and official prestige to bring about compliance or at least to make the role of resistance more difficult.

Instead, the President gave verbal aid and comfort to the leaders of resistance. He expounded theories of federalism more restrictive of national power than those of Chief Justice Waite and Justice Bradley, ideas of the role of law in race relations similar to those of Justice Brown, and conceptions of the presidency closer to those of James Buchanan than those of Washington, Jackson, or Lincoln. Thus the President repeatedly stressed the responsibility of state and local officials to enforce desegregation orders of the federal courts, the inefficacy of law as a means of social control in race relations, and the impropriety of his expression of approval and disapproval of the decision of 1954. In so doing, usually in impromptu answers to reporters' questions, President Eisenhower condemned with equal impartiality as extremists Negroes having recourse to legal processes to vindicate their rights and resistance groups resorting to lawlessness to suppress constitutional rights; he uncritically and unintentionally equated the bombing of a school to a leaking faucet; and he urged a slower approach to school desegregation.[54]

[54] See especially the transcripts of the President's news conferences of September 4, 1956, and September 3, 1957. Among other typical utterances are those in press conferences of November 23, 1954; March 14, August 18, and September 11, 1956; July 17 and October 3, 1957; July 3 and August 6 and 20, 1958; January 14 and 21, May 13, and July 8, 1959. It should be noted that even though President Eisenhower has taken a

With neither the President nor Congress having a policy or a plan for meeting the constitutional crisis in race relations, the burden of implementing the Supreme Court decision has fallen almost exclusively on the federal judiciary, and primarily on the United States district courts. Accordingly, one of the most important policies of social change in the twentieth century was committed to the tedious and fortuitous process of private litigation, with the final judgment affecting only the parties in controversy. The relative inadequacy of judicial precedents as vehicles for social change, in contrast to the efficiency of legislation and administration to effectuate change rapidly, has long been a theme of text writers in jurisprudence, who are amply corroborated by the rough figures cited above and the events that have occurred in the area of race relations since May, 1954.

The decisions of the Court aimed at the attainment of equality before the law, inadequate as they are when standing alone, are, nevertheless, in accord with the trend of history noted by de Tocqueville in 1835, when he wrote that there was scarcely a single event of the preceding seven hundred years that did not promote equality of condition,[55] and then declared: "The gradual development of the principle of equality is, therefore, a providential fact . . . it is universal, it constantly eludes all interference, and all events as well as all men contribute to its progress." [56] It may be that the passion for equality, as Justice Holmes thought, is "an ignoble aspiration" and the idealization of envy,[57] but it is certain, as

---

Trappist vow of silence concerning his thoughts on the merits of the 1954 decision, he did at a news conference on July 8, 1959, declare that segregation is morally wrong when it interferes with equality of opportunity in economic and political fields.

[55] Alexis de Tocqueville, *Democracy in America*, ed. Phillips Bradley (2 vols., New York, 1945), I, 5.

[56] *Ibid.*, 6.

[57] Mark DeWolfe Howe (ed.), *Holmes–Laski Letters*, (2 vols., Cambridge, Mass., 1953), I, 769; II, 942.

de Tocqueville asserted, that the passion for equality in democracies is "ardent, insatiable, incessant, invincible." [58] And though men may easily attain a certain equality of condition, they can never attain as much as they desire.[59]

In these times it would perhaps be well for both the advocates and the adversaries of equality to ponder de Tocqueville's conclusion to his great work, which was written to provide an example of equality to France: "The nations of our time cannot prevent the conditions of men from becoming equal, but it depends upon themselves whether the principle of equality is to lead them to servitude or freedom, to knowledge or barbarism, to prosperity or wretchedness." [60] To date, at least, the quest for equality in America has led to freedom, knowledge, and prosperity and has been marked by the raising of lower orders, and not by the levelling of higher ones.

[58] De Tocqueville, *Democracy in America*, II, 97.
[59] *Ibid.*, 138.   [60] *Ibid.*, 334.

Index of Cases

162

Subject Index

Abolitionists, 22–23, 30, 33; on equality and national rights, 17–18
Adams, John, 19
Adams, Samuel, on equality, 14
Aliens, and equal protection, 95–96
American Revolution, political theory of, 1, 43
Arnold, Thurman W., 69

Barker, Sir Ernest, 4 n., 8
Bayard, Thomas F., 50
Bickel, Alexander M., 26 n.
Bingham, John A., 22, 26 n., 32–34, 35, 36, 39–40, 44, 45–46, 47, 55, 84; on equality and natural rights, 18; on power of Congress to protect rights, 37–38
Black, Hugo, 68, 78, 79, 112, 113, 114, 115, 119, 121, 122, 127, 147 n.
Black Codes, 25, 40, 50
Blackstone, Sir William, 22, 27 n., 29
Blair, Francis P., Jr., 50
Blair, James G., 48–49
Boyer, Benjamin M., 146 n.

Bracton, Henry of, 2
Bradley, Joseph, 74, 83–84, 85, 91, 145, 156; on state action, 86; and narrow construction of civil rights, 87–88
Bradley, Phillips, 157 n.
Brandeis, Louis D., 70 n.
Brewer, David J., 73
Broomall, John M., 29
Brown, Henry Billings, 136, 156; on separate but equal formula, 98–101
Buchanan, James, 156
Burgess, John W., 82–83 n.
Burton, Harold, 121
Butler, Pierce, 71
Byrd, Harry, 155

Calhoun, John C., 22, 29, 150
Cardozo, Benjamin N., 70 n., 118, 149
Carlyle, A. J., 3, 5 n., 7, 9 n.
Carlyle, Sir Robert W., 7
Carpenter, Matt H., 49, 73–74
Cash, Wilbur J., 98 n.
Cater, Douglass, 125 n.
Catron, John, 20 n.
Chain stores, discriminatory taxes on, 71–72

Other Published Volumes of

THE EDWARD DOUGLAS WHITE

LECTURES ON CITIZENSHIP

Education for Freedom
    by Robert M. Hutchins

Liberty Against Government
    by Edward S. Corwin

*Morality and Administration
in Democratic Government*
    by Paul H. Appleby

The States and the Nation
    by Leonard D. White

A Larger Concept of Community
    by Jefferson B. Fordham

*Individual Freedom and
Governmental Restraints*
    by Walter Gellhorn

*The Supreme Court from
Taft to Warren*
    by Alpheus Thomas Mason

The Quest for Equality
    by Robert J. Harris